Kennette a

# How to Have
# CONFIDENCE AND POWER
# in Dealing with People

# How to Have
# CONFIDENCE AND POWER
## in Dealing with People

by

## Les Giblin

Englewood Cliffs, N. J.
PRENTICE-HALL, INC.

Twenty-fifth Printing..........May, 1972

PRINTED IN THE UNITED STATES OF AMERICA
41068—B&P

To My Wife GRETCHEN
and My Mother ELIZABETH

whose inspiration, guidance, and
help made this book possible

# CONTENTS

## Part One

## MAKING HUMAN NATURE WORK FOR YOU

Part Two

HOW TO CONTROL THE ACTIONS AND
ATTITUDES OF OTHERS

# CONTENTS

## Part Five

# HOW TO MANAGE PEOPLE SUCCESSFULLY

# CONTENTS

## Part Six

## YOUR HUMAN RELATIONS WORKBOOK

# WHAT THIS BOOK CAN DO FOR YOU

# WHAT THIS BOOK CAN DO FOR YOU

LET'S BE HONEST ABOUT IT: WE DO WANT THINGS from other people. We want other people's good will and friendship. We want their acceptance and recognition.

A businessman wants business from other people. A husband and wife want love and affection from each other. A parent wants obedience. A child wants security and love. A salesman wants other people to sign their names on a dotted line. A boss wants loyalty, production, cooperation. An employee wants recognition and credit for what he does.

Every normal human being wants success and happiness. Have you ever thought about the fact that other people play an important part in any real success or happiness that we enjoy? It is largely through our dealings with other people that we become successful. And regardless of what your definition of happiness may be, a little thought will convince you that your own happiness is largely dependent upon the sort of relationships you have with other people.

### *Why not go after what you want?*

Let's not apologize for the fact that we need what other people have to offer. Let's not apologize for the fact that we want to be successful in our dealings with others.

Instead, let's get together in this book and have a heart-to-heart talk about how you can go about getting what you want from other people.

I have no Pollyanna theories about how people ought to act, and no gimmicks or gizmoes for getting along with others by keeping down your own desires.

Instead, I want to tell you in this book some things I have discovered about how human beings *do* act and react, and how you can use these things to get what you want, whether it is a raise from your boss, an order from a prospect, or good will from a new neighbor.

It has been said that "Knowledge is power." Knowledge about human nature *as it is*—not as theorists say it *ought* to be—can help you get what you want from other people.

The methods presented in this book do not represent any high-flung theories that I dreamed up, but represent *tested methods and techniques* that grew out of many years' work in my human relations clinics. They have proved themselves in the lives of thousands of people.

These methods may upset some popular ideas.

But they do have one advantage: They work!

### Everybody wins; nobody loses

Thousands of people know that they want things from other people. But they are timid in going after what they want in the fear that satisfying their own desires would be selfish. They instinctively feel that securing success and happiness for themselves would necessarily mean depriving some other human being of some success or happiness.

Let's get one thing straight: successful human relations means giving the other fellow something he wants in return for something you want. Any other method of dealing with people simply doesn't work. The reader who has no scruples about taking what he wants from other people without giving something in return does not need a book on human relations.

This book is written for those thousands of people who would like to master the art of getting what they want from the other fellow — and making the other fellow happy about it.

## *The three basic methods of dealing with people*

No human being is self-sufficient. Each of us needs things that other people have to offer. You have things that other people need. All our dealings with other people are based upon these needs. There are only three basic ways in which we deal with other people:

1. You can take what you need from the other fellow by force, threats, intimidation, or by outsmarting him. Although criminals naturally fall in this category, many respectable people employ this method in more subtle ways.
2. You can become a human relations beggar, and beg other people to give you the things you want. This submissive type of personality makes a deal with other people: "I won't assert myself in any way or cause you any trouble, and in return you be nice to me."
3. You can operate upon a basis of fair exchange, or give-and-take. You make it your business to give other people things they want and need, and invariably they will turn around and give you the things you need.

## *How to tap your unused assets*

You won't find anything in this book about the first two methods mentioned above. Instead, you will learn tested methods for getting what *you* want by giving other people what *they* want.

Right now you have in abundance many things that other people want. Offer these things to other people and they will gladly give you success and happiness in return. Maybe you have never fully realized that you possess valuable assets that other people are hungry for. I want to tell you about these assets in this book.

## *You can get what you want and help others at the same time*

For many years, we have assumed that if we attempted to satisfy our own desires for success and happiness, we would of necessity deprive some other person of satisfying his own wants. But the evidence all points in the other direction.

A happy human being is more likely to spread happiness than an unhappy human being. A prosperous human being is more likely to benefit those with whom he deals than is a chronic failure. A person who has reasonably satisfied his own desires is much more generous and considerate in taking into account the desires of others than is a person whose every desire has been frustrated.

Psychologists, criminologists, ministers, and now even doctors tell us that most of the trouble and misery in this world is caused by *unhappy people*. They tell us that by making yourself miserable and frustrated, you are doing other people the greatest disservice you could possibly devise.

### The key to successful human relations

The real key to successful human relations is learning as much as we can about human nature *as it is,* not as we think it ought to be. Only when we understand just what we are dealing with are we in a position to deal with it successfully.

So let's take a look at human nature. Let's see just what it is that other people really want. Let's get together and work out some methods for supplying these needs and wants. Let's learn how to work *with* human nature, rather than *against* it.

Maybe we'll learn that the big trouble with the world isn't that people are made the way they are, but that we too often ignore the hungers of the people with whom we deal. You may be agreeably suprised to find that human nature really needs no glossing over, no idealizing, but that the good Lord really did know what He was doing when He made us the way He did.

Whenever I hear somebody knocking human nature, and blaming his troubles on the fact that the human race is so cussed, I am reminded of something that Harry Matelski, director of personnel for Wolf & Dessauer, Fort Wayne, Indiana, once said:

"Les," he remarked, "have you ever noticed that a mediocre typist is very likely to express dissatisfaction with the typewriter?

And that a poor golfer is always blaming a poor shot on his sorry golf clubs? You'll also find that people with little skill in human relations are the ones who are always cussing human nature— and blaming all their troubles on the fact that other people are so ornery."

### How you can have confidence and power in dealing with others

The real object of this book is to teach you how to have *confidence* and *power* in dealing with people.

One of the big reasons so many people lack confidence in dealing with others is that they do not understand what they are dealing *with*. We are always unsure of ourselves and lack confidence when we are dealing with the unknown. Watch a mechanic try to repair the engine of a strange automobile that he does not understand. He hesitates. His every movement shows lack of confidence. Then watch a master mechanic, who understands the engine he is working with. His every movement exudes confidence. It is the same for *anything* we are dealing with. The more we know about it—the more confidence we will have in dealing with it.

Memorizing a few "rules" on human relations, which you apply as if they were gimmicks, won't give you confidence in dealing with people. But an understanding of human nature and an understanding of the basic principles behind human behavior will. Once you understand why people act as they do, you'll automatically find yourself feeling more *confident* in dealing with them.

Along with an understanding of human nature, this book will also give you definite practical methods to apply. You will be given *tested techniques* for putting into practice your knowledge of human nature. These tested techniques have worked for thousands of others, and they will work for you. Once you begin to *put into practice* your knowledge about people, you will find in yourself a new *power* in dealing with them.

### . . . Now let's get on to Chapter 1.

# How to Have
# CONFIDENCE AND POWER
## in Dealing with People

---

## Part One

# MAKING HUMAN NATURE WORK FOR YOU

---

# Chapter 1

# YOUR KEY TO SUCCESS AND HAPPINESS

---

$A$LL OF US WANT TWO THINGS OUT OF LIFE: *Success* and *Happiness*.

All of us are different. Your idea of success may be different from mine. But there is one *Big Factor* which all of us must learn to deal with if we are to be successful or happy. The *Big Factor* is the same whether you are a lawyer, doctor, businessman, salesman, parent, sales-clerk, housewife, or what-not.

The one *common denominator* to all success and happiness is *other people*.

Various scientific studies have proven that if you learn how to deal with other people, you will have gone about 85 per cent of the way down the road to success in any business, occupation, or profession, and about 99 per cent of the way down the road to personal happiness.

### Merely getting along isn't the answer

Merely learning how to get along with people is no guarantee of either success or happiness. The Caspar Milquetoasts in life have learned a way to get along with people to avoid trouble. The timid, retiring, doormat type of person has learned one way to "get along with people," *i. e.,* to simply let them walk over him.

On the other extreme, the tyrannical, dictator-like type of person also has worked out a way to "get along with people":

he simply beats down all opposition, *makes a doormat of them,* and proceeds to walk over them.

We don't need any more books on how to get along with people, for each of us already has his private system all worked out. Even the neurotic has his own special way of doing this, and psychologists tell us that neurosis itself can be defined as a pattern of responses which the neurotic has worked out for getting along with people.

What counts is a way to get along with people, or deal with people, that will bring us *personal satisfaction* and at the same time not trample on the egos of those we deal with. Human relations is the science of dealing with people in such a way that our egos and their egos remain intact. And this is the *only* method of getting along with people that ever brings any real success or any real satisfaction.

### The reason 90 per cent of people fail in life

The Carnegie Institute of Technology analyzed the records of 10,000 persons, and arrived at the conclusion that 15 per cent of success is due to technical training, to brains and skill on the job, and 85 per cent of success is due to personality factors, to the ability to deal with people successfully!

When the Bureau of Vocational Guidance at Harvard University made a study of thousands of men and women who had been fired, they found that for every one person who lost his job for failure to do the work, two persons lost their jobs for failure to deal successfully with people.

The percentage ran even higher in a study reported by Dr. Albert Edward Wiggam, in his syndicated column, "Let's Explore Your Mind." Out of 4,000 persons who lost their jobs in one year, only 10 per cent or 400 lost out because they could not do the work. Ninety per cent, or 3,600 of them, lost out because they had not developed the personality for successfully dealing with other people!

### Where success and happiness come from

Look around you. Are the most successful people you know

those with the most brains, the most skill? Are the people who are the happiest and get the most fun out of life so much smarter than the other people you know? If you will stop and think a minute, the chances are that you will say that the people you know who are the most successful, and enjoy life the most, are those who "have a way" with other people.

### Your personality problems are your problems with other people

There are millions of people today who are self-conscious, shy, timid, ill-at-ease in social situations, who feel inferior and never realize that their *real* problem is a human relations problem. It never seems to get across to them that their failure as a personality is really a failure in learning to deal successfully with other people.

There are almost as many who, at least on the surface, seem to be the very opposite of the shy, retiring type. They appear to be self-assured. They are "bossy" and dominate any social group they are in, whether it is the home, the office, or the club. Yet they too realize that something is missing. They wonder why their employees or their families do not appreciate them. They wonder why other people don't cooperate more willingly, why it is necessary to continually force people into line. And most of all, they realize in their more candid moments that the people they are most anxious to impress never really give them the approval and acceptance that they crave. They attempt to force cooperation, to force loyalty and friendship, to force people to produce for them, but the one thing they cannot force is the thing they want the most. They cannot force other people to like them, and they never really get what they want because they have never mastered the art of dealing with other people.

Bonaro Overstreet, in her book *Understanding Fear in Ourselves and Others,** says that disruptive emotional problems *always* have their root in our relations with other people. "The human being experiences fear when his car skids on an icy high-

---

* New York: Harper and Brothers, 1951.

way; but such fear does not distort his personality. He experiences pain when he drops a hammer on his foot; but such pain does not foster a brooding hostility. . . The one loss he cannot tolerate and remain in emotional health is loss of good will between himself and his fellow humans."

### Horse-and-buggy methods won't work in an atomic age

There might have been a time in past history when a prominent industrialist could say "The people be damned" and get away with it. Even as recently as World War II, when consumer goods were scarce, salesmen, sales-clerks, and businessmen could get by with a similar attitude.

Back before the "emancipation of women," human relations in the home were also a simple matter. The husband and father simply played the role of lord and master; if he brought it off, there was little trouble, at least on the surface.

But times have changed, and people who are living in the past and trying to make horse-and-buggy methods work in an atomic age are being left by the wayside, far behind some jet-powered expert in modern-day human relations.

As civilization progresses, as new inventions shrink our world smaller and smaller, as our economic life becomes more specialized and complicated, *other people* become more and more important to us.

### Davy Crockett's world is no more

Davy Crockett was a rugged individualist, and could afford to be. In his day human beings were not as dependent upon each other as we are today. Whether he had a bear steak or warmed-over rabbit stew for supper depended largely upon his own inclination and the sharpness of his shooting eye. But whether Mrs. Giblin enjoys a choice cut of Grade A steak or not may very well depend upon her human relations with the corner butcher, and whether or not her husband has had any success in dealing with people during the past week.

Davy Crockett's skill in handling "Old Betsy" was almost all that he needed. But even technical skill in our modern world takes a back seat to skill in dealing with people. Let me give you a couple of examples:

### Human engineering more important than technical knowledge

If there is one profession today that would seem to be entirely a matter of technical skill, it is surely engineering. Yet Purdue University kept careful records of its engineering graduates over a period of slightly more than five years. The earnings of those who made the very highest marks in school—those who appeared to have really mastered all the technical details and to have had the brains to master their profession, were compared with the earnings of those who made the lowest marks. There was barely $200 per year difference.

But when the earnings of those graduates who had demonstrated a marked ability to deal with others in social situations were compared, it was found that they averaged about 15 per cent more than of those in the "smart" group, and about 33 per cent more than of those with low personality ratings.

It is ironic that today many people are very much interested in improving their personalities, but show little or no interest in human relations techniques. Yet, as Dr. Albert Edward Wiggam, the eminent psychologist, has pointed out, when you boil *personality* down to its basic ingredients, it is nothing more than the ability to *interest* and *serve* other people.

### People are here to stay

Whether we like it or not, people are here to stay. In our modern world we simply cannot achieve any success or happiness without taking other people into account.

The doctor, the lawyer, the salesman who enjoys the most success is not necessarily the man who is the most intelligent, or the most skillful in the mechanics of his job. The salesgirl who sells the most goods and has more fun doing it is not necessarily the most beautiful or the brainiest.

The husband and wife who are the happiest are not the ones with the prettiest faces or the most he-man physiques.

Look for a success in any line and you will find a man or woman who has mastered the knack of dealing with people— a person who has a "way" with others.

### Tested Methods for Getting What You Want

To me, this business of how to deal with people successfully has always been of tremendous interest. For years I studied the successful men and women I knew to try to see what made them tick. I also studied men and women who had failed, for the same reason. I read everything I could find on the subject, but I found that most of the books on "getting along with others" were not based on any accurate studies of how people behave and what people really want. Instead they consisted of some-one's pet ideas of how people *should* act, and what they "ought to" want. They were either Pollyanna-type essays on how to placate others by *giving up* every satisfaction you wanted for yourself, or else advice on how to dominate others by a "forceful personality."

Over a period of years, however, I found that there were men and women who were quietly using techniques and methods that *worked,* not only in getting along with other people, but in getting what they wanted as well.

Strangely enough, many of the methods and techniques used by these people were the same old techniques that had been written about for years, but with one big difference. They were applied, not superficially, or as "gimmicks," but with an *understanding of human nature.* They were used as *principles* rather than platitudes.

### Skill depends on mastering certain basic principles

Skill in human relations is similar to skill in any other field, in that success depends upon understanding and mastering certain basic general principles. You must not only know *what* to do, but *why* you're doing it.

*Don't be a Johnny-One-Note.* As far as basic principles are concerned, people are all the same. Yet each individual person you meet is different. If you attempted to learn some gimmick to deal successfully with each separate individual you met, you would be faced with a hopeless task, just as a pianist would be up against an impossible task if he had to learn each individual composition as something entirely new and unique.

What the pianist does is to master certain principles. He learns certain basic things about music. He practices certain exercises until he develops skill at the keyboard. When he has mastered these basic things, he can then play *any* piece of music that is put before him, with some practice and additional learning. For although each individual piece of music is different from every other—there are only 88 keys on the piano, and only eight notes in the scale.

Whether you are a pianist or not, you can quickly learn to strike a "pretty chord" on the piano. With a little more patience you can learn to strike separately all the separate chords that the concert pianist uses. But this does not make you a pianist. If you tried to give a concert you would be a flop.

*Influencing people is an art, not a gimmick.* In much the same way, this is what happens when you try to learn a few gimmicks of "influencing people" and apply them in a superficial, mechanical way. You go through the same motions as the man or woman who "has a way" with people, but somehow they don't seem to work for you. You hit the same notes but no music comes out.

The purpose of this book is not to teach you a few "chords," but to help you master the keyboard—not to teach you a few gimmicks of dealing with people but to give you "know-how" based upon an understanding of human nature and why people act the way they do.

The methods that are presented in this book have been *tested on thousands of people* who have attended my human relations clinic. They are not just my pet ideas of how you "ought to" deal with people, but ideas that have stood the test of how you *must* deal with people if you want to get along with them, and get what you want at the same time.

Yes, all of us want success and happiness. But the day is long past, if it ever existed, when you could get these two prizes by forcing people to give you what you want. Begging for what you want is no better, for no one has any respect for, or any desire to help, the person who constantly kowtows and literally goes around with his hand out, begging other people to like him.

The one successful way to get the things you want from life **is** to acquire skill in dealing with people.

### *CHAPTER 1 IN A NUTSHELL*

1. **It is a proven fact that from 66 to 90 per cent of all failures in the business world are failures in human relations.**
2. **So-called personality problems, such as timidity, shyness, and self-consciousness, are basically problems in dealing with people.**
3. **Learn skill in dealing with people with confidence and you will automatically improve your own success and happiness.**
4. **Learn the underlying principles involved in dealing with people and you won't need gimmicks.**

# Chapter 2

# HOW TO USE THE BASIC SECRET FOR INFLUENCING OTHERS

As I WRITE THIS, THE NEWSPAPERS CARRY TWO stories, seemingly unrelated. One has to do with a man who strangled a woman because she went to sleep while he was talking to her. The other has to do with a 17-year-old boy who, with two other companions, robbed a service station. The 17-year-old was afflicted with buck-teeth, and admitted that he had not *wanted* to rob, but that all his life other boys had poked fun at him, and he merely wanted prove to them that he was a "man."

Both these stories point out the extremes to which people will go to defend a wounded ego. You can injure a man physically, you can steal his goods, you can damage him in all sorts of ways, and get by with it. But the one unforgivable sin, as far as human relations are concerned, is to trample on another person's ego. The minute you detract from another's dignity as a human being, you are in for trouble.

Because the human ego is such a precious thing to its possessor, and because a person will go to such extremes to defend *what he thinks are threats* to his ego, the word *egotism* has become a bad word.

### Let's look at the other side of egotism

If egotism can admittedly cause people to do silly and irrational and destructive things, it can also cause them to act nobly and heroically.

11

What is egotism, anyway?

Edward Bok, famous editor and humanitarian, said that what the world calls ego and conceit is really a "divine spark" planted in man, and that only those men and women who had "lighted the divine spark within them" ever did great things.

Whatever name you want to give it—"human dignity," "personality," or what-not—there is something deep in the heart of every man and woman that *is* important and *demands* respect. Every human being is a unique, individual personality, and the most powerful drive in any person is to maintain this individuality, to defend this important something against all enemies.

This is why you cannot treat people as machines, as numbers on a register, or as "masses," and get by with it. Every effort that has been made to deprive human beings of this individual worth has failed. It is more powerful than armies and prison camps. It proved more powerful than the feudal lords who tried to turn people into serfs. It proved more powerful than Hitler's armies. And it set the stage for our own "land of the free"; for the Declaration of Independence, if you read it carefully, is really a declaration of independence for the *individual*. It derives its power not because it sets out certain rights for a certain *group* of men, but from the fact that it proclaims certain inalienable rights for "all men."

It is also well to note that our Declaration of Independence places the real worth of an individual as a gift of God, rather than as anything the individual has made of himself. "We hold these truths to be self-evident, that all men . . . are endowed by their Creator with certain unalienable Rights. . ."

This is not a book on religion. But, in the final analysis you cannot separate religion and human relations. Unless you believe that there is a Creator who has endowed men with unalienable rights, with an innate worth, you cannot very well believe in people. Communists claim that there is no Creator; hence, people are not very important to them either. The individual doesn't count to the Communist.

Henry Kaiser once said that you would *automatically* practice good human relations if you would remember that every individual *is* important, because every individual is a child of God.

This is also the only true basis for self-esteem. The man or woman who realizes that he is "something" not because of what he has done or how good he has been, but by the grace of God in endowing him with a certain innate worth, develops a healthy self-esteem. The man or woman who doesn't realize this tries to give himself significance by making money, gaining power, getting his name in the paper, or in a hundred other ways. Not only is he what we call an "egotist," when we use that word in its worst sense, but his continual unsatisfied hunger for self-esteem is what causes most of the trouble in this world.

## We are all egotists: four facts of life

If you are going to deal with people, whether they are children, wives, husbands, neighbors, bosses, workers, or convicts, you would do well to imprint the following indelibly on your mind, and act accordingly:

1.  We are all egotists.
2.  We are all more interested in ourselves than in anything else in the world.
3.  Every person you meet wants to feel important, and to "amount to something."
4.  There is a craving in every human being for the approval of others, so that he can approve of himself.

We are all ego-hungry. And it is only when this hunger is at least partially satisfied that we can "forget ourselves," take our attention off ourselves and give it to something else. It is only he who has learned to like himself who can be generous and friendly with other persons.

## What makes people self-centered and conceited?

We used to think that the trouble with the egotist was that he thought too highly of himself, that he had too much self-esteem, that if a person were self-centered, he should somehow give up his desire to think well of himself and he would be "cured." Even the old theoretical psychologists used to think that the egotist had too high an opinion of himself and that the way to deal with him was to "show him up," or "beat him down" and "knock some of his self-importance out of him." Hundreds of years ago, society tried these methods in dealing with criminals. Even to the present time, many individuals attempt to use these methods in dealing with contrary, hard-to-get-along-with people. However, such tactics have never worked. All they have ever succeeded in doing was to make the other person even more hostile, and to make his ego even more sensitive.

The reason these methods do not work is a simple one. Thanks to the work of clinical psychologists who have studied case histories of real people (not theoretical ones), we now know, without a doubt, that the self-centered, egotistical person is not suffering from too much self-esteem, but too little.

*If you're on good terms with yourself you're on good terms with others.* Bonaro Overstreet has even gone so far as to say that every single instance where an individual is at odds with himself and at odds with other people has proved to be a problem in lack of true self-esteem, and that the cure, in every case, consists in restoring self-esteem. Once a person begins to like himself a little better, then he is able to like other people a little better. Once he gets over his painful dissatisfaction with himself, he is less critical and more tolerant of others.

Clinical and experimental psychologists, after studying thousands of cases of *actual people* with all kinds of problems, came to the conclusion that ego-hunger is as universal and natural as the hunger for food. And food for the ego serves the same purpose as food for the body—self-preservation. The body needs food to survive. The ego, or unique individuality of each person, needs respect and approval and a sense of accomplishment.

*A starved ego is a mean ego.* Comparing the ego to the stomach goes a long way toward explaining why people act as they do. A man who eats three good meals a day gives little thought to his stomach. But let that man do without food for a day or two and become really hungry and his whole personality seems to change. From a generous, jolly, good-natured fellow, he is apt to become cantankerous and downright ornery. He becomes more critical. Nothing pleases him. He snaps at people. It will do no good for well-wishing friends to drop around and tell him that all his trouble is only that he is "stomach-conscious" and that he must get his mind off his stomach. Nor will it do any good to tell him that he should think less of himself and think more of others. There is but one way that he can get over his "stomach-centeredness" and that is to accede to nature's demand for survival. Nature has placed an instinct in each creature that says, "YOU and your basic needs come first." In short, he must eat, and take care of his own primary needs, before he is even capable of giving his attention to anything else.

It is very much the same with the self-centered person. For a healthy, wholesome, normal personality, nature demands a certain amount of self-acceptance and self-approval. And it does no good to scold a self-centered person and tell him to get his mind off himself. He *cannot* get his mind off his "self" until his ego-hunger has been satisfied. Then, he will indeed take his attention off his self, and give it to his work, and to other people and their needs.

### How to use LS/MFT

With apologies to the American Tobacco Company, let's consider how you can improve your relations with other people like magic, if you will remember the magic letters: *LS/MFT*. In this case, they stand for

**Low Self-Esteem Means Friction and Trouble.**

When self-esteem is at a high level, people are easy to get along with. They are cheerful, generous, tolerant, willing to listen to others' ideas. They have taken care of their own primary needs —and are able to think about the needs of others. Their own personalities are so strong and secure that they can afford to take a few risks. They can afford to be wrong, occasionally. They can admit to themselves that they have made a mistake. They can even be criticized and slighted, and take it in their stride—for such things only make a small dent in their self-esteem, and they have plenty more left.

It is a well-known fact that the man-at-the-top is easier to deal with than small-fry. The story is told of a private in World War I who shouted "Put out that damn match," only to find to his chagrin that the offender had been General "Black Jack" Pershing. When he tried to stammer out his apology, General Pershing patted him on the back and said, "That's all right son; just be glad I'm not a second lieutenant."

The status of a general was not threatened by the remark of a private.

*You have to lower yourself to be petty.* When self-esteem is at a low ebb, trouble and friction come easily. And when self-esteem becomes *low enough,* almost anything can become a threat. This is what happens when a man strangles a woman because she went to sleep while he was talking. Had his self-esteem been high enough, the affront would not have assumed such important proportions to him. Had the 17-year-old boy had enough self-esteem, he would not have had to rob a service station to prove to his buddies that "he was a man."

To the person with low self-esteem, even a critical look or one harsh word can seem like a calamity. The so-called "sensative souls" who see some "dig" or double-meaning in even the most innocent remark are suffering from low self-esteem. The braggart, the show-off, and the blusterer are also suffering from low self-esteem.

*How to understand the bully.* Even the arrogant person, who attempts to "put you in your place" or make you feel inferior, is really suffering from a low opinion of himself. You can understand his behavior if you keep in mind two things: first, he needs desperately to increase his own self-importance and is attempting to do so by beating you down, and second, he is afraid. His self-esteem is at such a low ebb that he realizes that just about one good "take-down" by you would be sufficient to destroy it altogether. And although he doesn't know for a fact that you would take a poke at his self-importance, he *cannot afford to take that chance.* He can't approach you man-to-man, on an equal basis, with his defenses down, because the risk involved would be too great. The only safe strategy he can use is to put you in your place, before you put him in his—which he imagines to be pretty low on the totem pole.

If you will remember those letters: LS/MFT, it will help you deal with all these people who suffer from low self-esteem. Understanding why they act the way they do will help you develop a strategy for handling them.

Realizing that it is low self-esteem that causes friction and trouble, you will not add to the trouble by trying to beat these people down even more. You will avoid sarcastic, cutting remarks. You won't try to argue them down, for if you "win" the arguments, you will only further decrease their ebbing supply of self-esteem and make them harder to deal with than before. This is the psychology behind the well-known remark: "Win the argument and lose the sale."

### How to turn a lion into a lamb

There is only one effective way to deal with trouble-makers:

**Help the Other Fellow Like Himself Better**

Feed his hungry ego—and he will stop growling and snapping at you.

Remember that a hungry dog is a mean dog. Well-fed dogs seldom want to fight, and in the old days of pit fighting dogs were starved for a day or two before a match to make them mean. This secret of successful human relations works not only on trouble-makers, but also on normal folks. Anyone is more agreeable, more understanding, more cooperative—if you feed his ego . . . not with insincere flattery, but with genuine compliments and real praise.

Try looking for little things you can compliment others on. Look for good points in those you deal with—points that you can praise them about. Form the habit of paying at least five sincere compliments each day—and watch how much smoother your relations with others become.

In Part Two of this book, we are going to get down to specific cases of just how you can *apply* this knowledge of human nature to everyday situations. But don't wait for the details. Begin right now to think up your own ways sincerely to HELP THE OTHER FELLOW LIKE HIMSELF BETTER. And do not attempt to apply this knowledge with a superior, patronizing manner. If you do, you will be seen through, and your presumption of superiority will only antagonize.

Remember this first law of human relations, as you read the remainder of this book. You will see it running through many of the case histories to be presented later, and it will enable you to understand why the various methods presented do work.

*The First Law of Human Relations* might be summarized: "People act—or fail to act—largely to enhance their own egos." When you are trying to persuade another person to act in a certain way, and logic and reason seem to fail, try giving him a "reason" that will enhance his ego. We are often told to "appeal to reason" and to "reason with children." But when it comes to getting people to act in a certain way—the word *reason* means a "reason that will enhance the ego."

### The same principle works on children or kings

It works with wives. It works with husbands, children, waitresses, hotel desk clerks—even with kings.

When General Oglethorpe wanted permission from the King of England to found a colony in the New World, he tried, for many weeks, all sorts of "logical arguments" on the King. The King wasn't interested. Oglethorpe appealed to his humanity, and made all sorts of appeals with what he considered good "reasons." But the King was not moved by them. Finally, Oglethorpe decided to change his strategy. At his next audience with the King, Oglethorpe started out trying to sell the idea of what a fine thing it would be for England to have a colony in the New World—what a glorious thing it would be to plant the English flag in new territory.

"But we already *have* colonies in the New World," said the King.

"True, Sire," said Oglethorpe, "but none of them is named for you."

The King sat up and took notice. He not only gave permission to settle the new colony named Georgia, he financed the whole thing and even helped to populate it by setting scot-free debtors who owed money to the Crown.

### Give the other fellow a personal reason to help you

Not long ago I was in a southern city where there was a national convention going on, and unexpected business developments required that I stop overnight. I went around to a hotel where I had previously stayed, and finally worked my way through the crowd that was standing around the desk trying to get rooms.

"Gosh, Les," the desk clerk apologized. "You should have let us know you were coming. I'm afraid there isn't anything I can do for you under the circumstances."

"It sure looks like we've got a problem," I responded, "but I know that if there's any hotel man in town who can lick it— it's you. And there's no need in my looking any further, because if *you* can't get me a room I might as well plan to sleep in the park."

"Well," he said, "I don't know. But stick around about 30 minutes and let me see whether I can think of anything or work something out."

The upshot was that he remembered there was a small living room, luxuriously furnished and usually used for informal conferences, that could easily be turned into a bedroom, complete with bath, by simply moving in a spare bed. I got the room, and he got a sense of accomplishment and enhanced his ego by proving to both of us that "If anybody can do it, *I* can do it."

### THE ESSENCE OF CHAPTER 2

1. We are all egotists.
2. We are all more interested in ourselves than in anything else in the world.
3. Every person you meet wants to feel important, and to amount to something.

4. There is a hunger in every human being for approval.
5. A hungry ego is a mean ego.
6. Satisfy the other person's hunger for self-esteem and he automatically becomes more friendly and likeable.
7. Jesus said, "Love thy neighbor as thyself." Psychologists now tell us that unless you *do* love yourself in the sense of having some feeling of self-esteem and self-regard, it is impossible for you to feel friendly toward other people.
8. Remember L S / M F T. Low Self-esteem Means Trouble and Friction.
9. Help the other fellow like himself better and you make him easier to get along with.
10. People act, or fail to act, largely to enhance their own egos.

# Chapter 3

# HOW TO CASH IN ON YOUR HIDDEN ASSETS

---

Every human being is a millionaire in human relations. The great tragedy is that too many of us hoard this wealth, or dole it out stingily. Or worse still, don't even realize we possess it.

During World War II, when people were hungry for meat, and meat was scarce, the butcher became the most popular man in the community.

Yet, every day of your life the people with whom you come into contact are hungry and thirsty for food that you could give them.

One of the most universal hungers is the hunger to feel important, to have your personal worth as a human being confirmed by others, to be appreciated, to be noticed.

It is within your power to add to the feeling of personal worth of the other person. It is within your power to make him like himself a little better. It is within your power to make him feel appreciated and accepted.

In short, you have the bread to feed this human hunger.

## Try giving away your wealth

The quickest way to improve your human relations is to begin giving away this wealth that you possess. Don't be stingy with it. Don't dole it out. Don't play any favorites. It doesn't cost you anything, and you need not fear you'll ever use it all

21

up. Don't try to barter or bargain with it. Don't try to use it to bribe people into giving you what you want. Give it away indiscriminately; in doing so, you need not worry about getting what you want from others. But when you cast this bread upon the waters, so to speak, it always comes back to you multiplied many fold.

### Everyone is hungry for this food

Do not make the mistake of supposing that just because a man is successful or famous, he has no need for a feeling of importance.

Courtesy, politeness, and what we call "manners," are all based upon this universal hunger of people to feel that they have some personal worth.

Courtesy and politeness are merely ways in which we *acknowledge* the importance of the other person.

Remember the headlines when a premier of a foreign country called to keep an appointment with a cabinet officer in Washington, had to find his own way to the office, was required to give his name to the cabinet officer's secretary, and was then kept waiting five minutes past the time of the appointment? Remember what a stir it caused in diplomatic circles when the premier quietly left at the end of five minutes, saying, "We will see him later"?

Was his time so valuable that he could not afford to wait five minutes? Probably not. Was it possible that months of hard work towards establishing good relations with this foreign country could all be cancelled by such a small thing. Apparently the experts thought so, considering the way they scurried around to straighten things out.

*A quality you have in common with everyone else in the world.* Every person reading this book is different from the next person reading it. You live differently, eat differently, dress differently, like different things—you are different. But there is one thing we all have in common.

All of us not only need to feel that we are important: *We need to feel that other people recognize and acknowledge our im-*

*portance.* Actually, what we need is for other people to *help* us feel important—help us confirm our sense of personal worth. For our own feelings about ourselves are to a large extent the *reflections* of the feelings other people have, or seem to have, about us. Not one man in a million can long maintain his feeling of dignity and worth, so necessary to his well-being, if everyone he meets treats him as if he were a "nobody" and worthless.

This explains why so-called "little things"—little, apparently unimportant actions—can have such tremendous consequences in the field of human relations.

After all, you may say, what is five minutes? Actually, the five minutes time—as time—was not important at all. What was important was what the five minutes said—under the circumstances. To be kept waiting five minutes said, or seemed to say—"This meeting is not very important to me. I consider meeting with you more or less a routine affair. I do not place much value on seeing you."

Have you ever read the so-called reasons people give for asking for divorce? Some of them seem almost funny.

"He always ogled pretty women every time he took me out."

"He got a big kick out of telling everyone how stupid I was about money."

"She deliberately burned my toast every morning, just because she knew I hated burned toast."

"She would make an issue of feeding the cat before she fed me."

They *seem* like small things. But when they are endlessly repeated, and keep saying to the other person, "This proves I don't think you are very important"—then they become truly "tremendous trifles."

Remember, it takes only one small spark to set off a tremendous explosion. And the little things you do or say can cause a chain reaction that becomes atomic.

### You must "recognize" the other person

In their diplomatic dealings with other countries, governments speak of "recognizing" another country, or "according them recognition." "Recognition" means that the other country is considered to be a bona fide, "real" government.

We might well take a lesson from this in our diplomatic relations with other human beings. For to be successful in deal-ing with others, we too must "recognize" them as a bona fide, "real" human beings.

J. C. Staehle, after analyzing many surveys, found that the principal causes of unrest among workers were the following, listed in the order of their importance:

1. Failure to give credit for suggestions
2. Failure to correct grievances
3. Failure to encourage
4. Criticizing employees in front of other people
5. Failure to ask employees their opinions
6. Failure to inform employees of their progress
7. Favoritism

Notice that every single item has to do with failure to recog-nize the importance of the employee. Failure to give credit for work says, "Your work isn't very important." Failure to correct grievances says, "You are so unimportant that your grievances don't amount to anything," and so on.

### Three Ways to Make People Feel Important

#### 1. Think other people are important

The first rule of all—and the easiest to apply—is simply to convince yourself once and for all that other people *are* im-portant. Do this, and your own attitude gets across to the other fellow—even when you are not "trying." Moreover, it takes away the need for "gimmicks" and puts your human relations on a sincere basis. You can try rules and gimmicks until you are blue in the face, and they won't work for you, if you do them with your tongue in your cheek. You can't make the other fel-low feel important in your presence if you secretly feel that he is a nobody.

After all, what else on earth *is* as important as people? What is as interesting?

*One big reason why everybody is important.* Earlier in this book we mentioned what Henry Kaiser calls the number one rule for getting along harmoniously with other people: simply recognizing that every single person you meet is a child of God, and that makes him important.

Dr. J. B. Rhine of Duke University has said pretty much the same thing in more scientific language. Dr. Rhine and his associates, over a period of more than 20 years, made scientific experiments which prove that there is something "extra-physical" about man. In other words, the scientists are telling us that they have proved by controlled experiments that man is more than a flesh-and-blood machine, that he is more than just a physical "animal."

Dr. Rhine says that when these findings are generally recognized and accepted they will change our dealings with each other for the better. In his book, *The Reach of the Mind,* * he says:

"Our treatment of people obviously depends on *what we think they are,* as does our treatment of everything else. No other way would be intelligent. Our feelings for men depend on our ideas, our knowledge about them. The more we are led on the one hand to think of our fellowmen as deterministic physical systems—robots, machines, brains—the more heartlessly and self-ishly we can allow ourselves to deal with them.

"On the other hand, the more we appreciate their mental life as something unique in nature, something more original and creative than the mere space-time-mass relations of matter, the more we are interested in them as individuals, and the more we tend to respect them and consider their viewpoints and feelings. Our interpersonal dealings are elevated to a level of mutual interest, of understanding, of fellowship."

Men and women who have the most influence with other people are men and women who *believe* other people are important.

---

* New York: William Sloane Associates, Inc., 1947.

## 2. Notice other people

Here again is a simple but basic rule.

Have you ever thought about the fact that you "notice" only those things that are important to you? Actually you never see a hundreth part of what is around you—you select for attention only those things that are important. Five people taking a Sunday afternoon stroll down the same street will probably "see" or notice five different things, simply because they are interested in different things. A visiting merchant notices the shops and mentally calculates the rent each must pay. A paving contractor notices the condition of the pavement and sees that it is in a sad state of repair. His wife notices the new frocks in the shop windows. His eight-year-old boy sees the pigeons and wishes he had brought his slingshot, and so on.

*How to make people work harder.* Subconsciously, we all know that we notice only what is important to us.

Therefore, when someone "notices" us, he pays us a big compliment. He is saying that he recognizes our importance. He gives a big boost to our morale. We become more friendly, more cooperative, and actually work harder.

Psychologists at the University of Michigan's Survey Research Center in Ann Arbor, Michigan, began a scientific study in 1949 which is still going on. They wanted to find what makes people work harder, what makes them produce more and do better work. They have found that the foreman who is interested in the people working under him gets more work from them than the bossy type who tries to force them to work harder.

"Science Newsletter," in reporting on the findings of these scientists,* said, "Pressuring for production may work to some degree. But the best results are achieved when a worker's internal motivations are tapped—his self-expression, self-determination, and sense of personal worth. A person works better when he is treated as a personality, given some degree of freedom in the way he does his work, and allowed to make his own decisions."

*How to hold people.* During World War II, labor turnover

---
* "Science Newsletter", April 16, 1949.

at the Harwood Manufacturing Corporation plant at Marion, Virginia was high. Getting people to stick on the job was a problem. To solve it the president called in a psychologist. The psychologist, wise in the ways of human nature, set up a program to *give individual attention* to new employees and make them feel that their significance was recognized by the company.

First, the new employee was interviewed by a personnel man who explained to him the general over-all picture of plant production and how his own job fitted into that picture. Next, he was given over to a "man-on-the-job" counselor who acted as the new worker's buddy. He explained his job to him, introduced him to the "fellows" and taught him the "ropes." Under this plan labor turnover dropped almost to zero!

*One secret for getting along with children.* Little children crave to be noticed. "Look, mama, look!" and, "Daddy, come watch me," are familiar phrases to all parents. Little Johnny isn't happy just going for a swim. He wants Daddy to "come watch me swim." These cries for notice are direct.

But often children ask for notice in more subtle ways. Little Susie may find that the one sure way to get her mother to notice her and pay individual attention to her is to refuse to eat when she comes to the table. And if, in spite of all efforts, Johnny's mama and daddy refuse to "look," he may go to needless extremes—such as knocking over a lamp, or twisting his sister's arm.

*How to cure naughtiness in children.* Dr. Ruth Barbee, well-known family-relations expert, tells me that about 90 per cent of so-called "naughtiness" in small children is simply their way of getting "noticed," when they cannot get the attention they want in any other way. And, she says, most naughtiness, and a great many so-called "bad habits" such as thumb-sucking and enuresis, can be cured quickly and simply by giving more time and attention to the child.

Criminologists say that many crimes, especially sensational ones, are performed by people who never had satisfied their craving for being noticed. The criminal goes out and does something spectacular which will make front-page headlines and says to himself, "Now, I guess the world will sit up and take notice of me."

*The most common complaint of wives and husbands.* Every

now and then someone takes a poll of husbands and wives to see what are the most common complaints that spouses have against each other.

Invariably, "not being noticed," in one form or another, heads the list. Many husbands cannot understand why a wife will have her feelings hurt because he does not notice her new hat or new hairdo. But the wife knows that his failure to notice the new hat means that he has not really looked at her—that he has not really paid any special attention to her. This, in turn, means that he does not consider her important enough to notice closely.

*How to make your customers like you.* One of the most successful sales-clerks I know never asks a woman "What size do you wear?"

Instead, she looks at the customer closely and says, "Let's see —you must take about a size 14." The customer feels good because she is being noticed, but doesn't quite know why. If the customer is a fat lady who would take a size 46, the sales-clerk, always "guesses" about two sizes too small. When the customer says, "No, I take a 46," the clerk says with surprise—"Well I would never have guessed it."

Here, she uses the same rule in reverse, by *not noticing* something that will detract from the feeling of importance of the other person.

*Turn the spotlight on everyone.* When you are dealing with a group, try to pay attention to everybody in the group, insofar as it is practical. If you are dealing with a man who is accompanied by his wife, pay *some attention* to the wife. Don't overdo it and direct all your remarks to her, for that would make her husband feel small. But don't ignore her either. Show that you *recognize* her presence. She will then help you sell your ideas to her husband.

If you are dealing with a committee or other group of persons, remember at least to acknowledge their presence as individuals. Look at them when they are talking and when you are talking. Again, don't overdo it. If you do you will detract from the importance of the chairman or leader of the group. Add to his self-importance by letting him know you recognize him as leader. But the chances are that you will need the support and good-will of a majority of the entire group, not just the leader. It is surprising what a small amount of attention to each individual is required in order to make him feel that you consider him important.

### 3. Don't lord it over people

The third basic rule for letting the other fellow know that you recognize his importance is one that requires some care. Because *you* are a human being and *you* have the same need to feel important that everyone else does, you must watch yourself to see that you do not use this basic fact about human nature to your own disadvantage.

The basic fact of human nature with which we are dealing is simply, "Everybody needs to feel important and feel that other people recognize his importance." This trait of human nature in itself is neutral. You can use it for your own advantage or disadvantage—just as you can use a knife to butter your bread or to cut your own throat.

The temptation is always present, when we are dealing with others, to impress upon them our own importance. Consciously or unconsciously, we want to make a good impression, too! If someone tells of some great feat he performed, we at once think of something we did that was even greater. If someone tells a good story, right away, we think of one that could top it. Often, we are so anxious to impress the other fellow with our own importance that we set out to make him feel small, so that it will make us appear bigger. "My daddy can lick your daddy," says little Jimmy Smith. And Jimmy's daddy is apt to make the same mistake, but in other words, in talking to the neighbor down the street.

There is one simple rule that will help you get over this handicap. Just remember this tried and proven fact:

**You Want to Make a Good Impression on the Other Fellow. But the Most Effective Way Ever Discovered for Impressing the Other Fellow Is to Let Him Know That *You Are Impressed by Him.***

Let him know that *he* impresses *you* and he will judge you one of the smartest, most personable individuals he ever met. Try to lord it over him—answer him with an "Oh yeah," or "You don't expect me to believe that, do you?" and he will be firmly convinced that you are a fool who doesn't know his way around.

Young Joe Doakes is dating two girls. One of them sits and listens to him tell about his job, his ambitions, what he has done and wants to do, and is terribly interested. She sits almost open-mouthed, and says, "How wonderful," or "How in the world did you do it?" The second girl says, "Oh, that isn't so great. I could do better than that myself."

Which girl is going to make the better impression? Which one is Joe going to think is the smarter of the two?

Giving the other person a feeling of importance—letting him know you are impressed—doesn't mean that anything will be taken away from you. It doesn't mean either, that you should fawn on him, kowtow to him, or become servile. It simply means that you should respect him, make him feel that he belongs.

*How to know when to correct another.* Usually when we contradict or correct another person, it is not for the purpose of settling any real problems—but only to increase our feeling of importance at the expense of someone else.

Another good rule to employ is to ask yourself, before you contradict someone, this question: "Does it make any *real* difference whether he is right or wrong?"

If he says the gun isn't loaded, and you know it is, contradict him.

If he says the bottle contains nail polish and you know it contains nitroglycerin, correct him.

But if he says it is 83 million miles to the sun, what real difference does it make if the figure is incorrect unless you are an astronomer or mathematician and the exact figure will make a difference in your problem.

*Don't try to win all the little battles.* Not long ago I had dinner with the owner of a small restaurant and a prominent accountant. During the conversation the restaurant man said, "I don't try to make too much money, because if you make $100,000 you are in the 90 per cent bracket and the government will only let you keep $10,000, while if you make only $30,000 you get to keep $15,000."

I looked at the accountant. He didn't bat an eyelash.

Afterwards, I said to him, "Why didn't you set him straight?"

"I'm surprised I have to tell you that, Les," he said. "I didn't set him straight simply because it would have served no purpose except to make him feel small. What difference does it really make whether he is set straight or not. He *wants* to believe that. If he made $100,000 a year and I was preparing his income tax returns I would set him straight, but since he doesn't make $100,000 and nothing is involved except his own ego—why bother?"

## POINTS TO REMEMBER IN CHAPTER 3

1. Don't be stingy in feeding the hunger for a feeling of importance.
2. Don't underestimate "small courtesies" such as being on time for an appointment. It is by such small things that we acknowledge the importance of the other person. Unfortunately, we are often more courteous to strangers than to home folks. Try treating your family and friends with the same courtesy you show strangers.
3. Remind yourself that other people *are* important, and your attitude will get across to the other person.
4. Starting today, begin to notice other people more. Pay attention to a man or a child, and you make him feel important.
5. Don't lord it over other people, or attempt to increase your own feeling of self-importance by making other people feel small.

# Part Two

# HOW TO CONTROL THE ACTIONS AND ATTITUDES OF OTHERS

---

Chapter 4

# HOW YOU CAN CONTROL THE ACTIONS AND ATTITUDES OF OTHERS

---

REMEMBER THE STORY OF SVENGALI, THE mesmerist who controlled the actions and behavior of others by a mysterious power?

It may surprise you to learn that each of us, in his way, is something of a Svengali . . . not that we have any such mysterious power as mesmerism over people. But each of us *already* exercises control over the actions and attitudes of other people. The only trouble is we do not *know* we are exercising this power, and we often use it against ourselves rather than for ourselves.

Some people may object to the idea of "controlling" the actions of others. But when you understand the law of psychology I want to tell you about in this chapter, you will see that we really have no choice. Each of us is constantly influencing and controlling the actions of those with whom we come into contact. The only choice we have is this: shall we use it for good or evil, for our benefit or our disadvantage?

For example, it may surprise you to learn that in about 95 per cent of the cases in which you are treated discourteously, snubbed, where someone else acts "unreasonably," you, yourself literally "asked for it." You were controlling the actions of the other person and in fact, *asking him to treat you discourteously.*

*How to adopt the attitude and action you want the other fellow to express*

There is a psychological law that makes human beings react and respond to the attitude and action expressed by the other fellow, in like manner. There is nothing mysterious about it, except the amazing results that come when you begin to put this law into effect. It makes sense. Everyone wants to do the appropriate thing. Everyone wants to "rise to the occasion." We act out our parts in life in accordance with the stage that we find set before us. There is an unconscious urge to "live up to" the opinions others seem to have of us, or to "live down" to them.

If you decide beforehand that a certain person is going to be difficult to deal with, chances are you will approach him in a more or less hostile manner, with your fists mentally clenched ready to fight. When you do this, you literally set the stage for him to act upon. He rises to the occasion. He acts the part that you have set for him to act, and you come away convinced that he really is a "tough customer," without ever realizing that your own actions and attitudes made him one.

In dealing with other people, we see our own attitudes reflected back to us in their behavior. It is almost as if you stood before a mirror. When you smile, the man in the mirror smiles. When you frown, the man in the mirror frowns. When you shout, the man in the mirror shouts back. Few people realize just how important and how predictable this law of psychology is. It is not just sweet talk about how people ought to act. It can be taken into a psychological laboratory and studied dispassionately and cold-bloodedly, just as any other natural law.

*When you're shouted at, you must shout back*

In conjunction with the U.S. Navy, the Speech Research Unit of Kenyon College proved that when a person is shouted at he simply cannot help but shout back, even when he cannot see the speaker.

Tests were made over telephones and intercoms to determine the best degree of loudness for giving instructions and commands. The speaker asked simple questions, each in a different degree of loudness. Invariably the answers came back in the same degree of loudness. When the question was soft, the answer that came back was soft. When the question was loud, the answer was loud.

The amazing fact that came out of the tests, however, was the discovery that the people on the receiving end *simply could not help* being influenced by the tones of the speaker. *No matter how hard they tried,* their own tones became louder or softer in exact proportion to the loudness or softness of the speaker's.

### How to control anger in others

You actually can use this scientific knowledge to keep another person from becoming angry, if you start in time. The technique is based on two well-known facts of psychology. One is the experiment we have just described: You control the other person's tone of voice by your own tone of voice. The other is this: Whether you talk loudly because you become angry, or whether you become angry because you talk loudly, is like asking "Which came first, the chicken or the egg?" It can happen either way. One thing is certain. The louder you talk, the angrier you become. Psychology has proved that if you *keep your voice soft you will not become angry.* Psychology has accepted as scientific the old Biblical injunction, "A soft answer turns away wrath."

Knowing these two facts, you can control the other person's emotions to an amazing degree. When you find yourself in an explosive situation—one of those "tense situations" that seems likely to get out of hand at almost any minute—deliberately lower the tone of your voice and keep it soft. This will literally force the other fellow to keep his own voice soft. And he can't become angry and emotional as long as he keeps his voice pitched in a soft tone. If you wait until the other person becomes angry, it won't work—but you can turn anger away before it arrives by using this technique.

### Enthusiasm is catching

Do you want others to become enthusiastic over your ideas,

the goods you are selling, your plans? Then remember the psychological law that says

### Adopt the Attitude and Action you Want the Other Fellow to Express.

Enthusiasm is more catching than the measles. So are indifference and lack of enthusiasm. Have you ever walked into a store where the clerks were draped lazily over the counters with a look of bored indifference on their faces? Have you ever asked a sales clerk a question about merchandise and have him answer you with a bored, "I don't know" which carried an implied "and furthermore I don't care."?

Chances are that you didn't like it, and left without buying anything—without quite knowing why. Analyze it, however, and you'll see that the clerk actually *made* you indifferent and took away whatever interest you might have had. Subconsciously you were saying to yourself, "Well, if the person who sells this merchandise isn't any more enthusiastic about it than this, it must not be worth my enthusiasm either."

*How to commit sales murder.* Recently I went into the sporting goods department of a large department store with the intention of buying a spinning reel and rod. I'm not much of a fisherman, but reading about the new spinning reels and hearing a few things about them, I became interested. My interest was quickly killed, however, by the lack of interest displayed by the clerk.

"Are these spinning outfits really all they are cracked up to be?" I asked.

"Oh, I guess so," he said. "Everybody to their own opinion."

"Don't you like them?"

"I don't know anything about them."

"Are they very popular?"

"Some people buy them. I just don't know. I understand they're good for an amateur because they won't backlash."

The end result was that I left without buying anything. "Must be having some trouble with them," I said to myself, "or he would have tried to sell me one."

A few weeks later I happened to be in Florida and had an opportunity to do a little fishing over a week-end. I went around to a small tackle shop and asked to be fixed up with a rig.

"Want a spinning outfit, I guess," said the old fellow behind the counter.

"Well, I don't know," I said. "Spinning is mostly for amateurs, isn't it?"

He fixed an unflinching eye on me and asked, "Mister, don't you like spin fishing?" as if he were surprised to death.

"Well," I replied, "I've never done any."

"Anybody that doesn't like spin fishing must have rocks in the head," he answered.

Now, that old man would never win any medals for diplomacy. But his utter and sincere enthusiasm for spin fishing completely cancelled the abruptness of his words. He was so completely "sold" himself that he sold me. All I could do was laugh and say, "Well, fix me up a spinning outfit."

> This brings up another phase of controlling the actions of other people. You never sell anything to anyone else until you yourself are sold on it. When you are sold, and the other fellow *knows* you are sold, he'll want it. Go one step further and sell yourself on the idea that *he is going to buy,* and he is almost *forced* into buying what you are selling.

The best testimony I have ever run across to prove that you can control the enthusiasm of others is Frank Bettger's book, *How I Raised Myself from Failure to Success in Selling.** Bettger was a failure until the age of 29. He almost starved to death when he first tried to make a living selling. Then he set out deliberately to make himself enthusiastic. He stopped trying to make others enthusiastic about his product by a direct frontal attack. Instead, he concentrated on *being* enthusiastic. And as he became enthusiastic—he found that others also became so and bought from him. He went on to become one of the most successful salesmen this country has ever produced.

---

* New York: Prentice-Hall, Inc., 1949.

*Confidence breeds confidence: how to make the most of it*

Just as you can make others enthusiastic by being enthusiastic, you can make others have confidence in you and in your proposition—by acting confidently.

It is a sad but true fact that many men of mediocre ability get further than others who have outstanding talents, merely because they know how to *act confidently.*

All the great leaders of men have known the importance of acting in a confident way. Napoleon, although perhaps not a good example of good human relations in many other ways, did know the magic of the confident manner and used it to an endless degree. After his first exile, when the French Army was sent out to get him, he didn't run or hide. Instead, he went out boldly to meet them. One man against an army. Yet, his supreme confidence that he was master of the situation worked magic. He acted as if he expected the army to take commands from *him,* and the soldiers marched back behind him.

*The Hilton story.* In his early years, Conrad Hilton had more confidence than money. In fact, about all he had in the way of assets was a reputation for keeping his word, and the ability to inspire in others the same confidence in his plans that he felt himself. No matter what the odds or obstacles, Hilton always *acted as if it were impossible to fail,* and his very manner, like magic, inspired others to believe that he could not fail. The first really first-class hotel Hilton ever owned was begun with less than $50,000 of his own money. When his mother came upon him drawing plans and asked what he was doing, he told her he was planning a really big hotel. "Where will the money come from," she asked.

"In here," said Hilton, tapping his head. By exhausting every possible source, he succeeded in raising about half-a-million dollars in capital. But when architects gave him an estimate for the hotel he wanted built, they said it would cost at least one million dollars. Without hesitation, he said "Draw up the plans."

Hilton then actually began building the hotel, without having the slightest idea where the money was going to come from to finish it. But because he himself not only talked of building a million dollar hotel—but actually acted as if he meant to do it—other people became convinced that "Connie can do it" and invested their money.

Henry Ford financed his company in its early days largely through using a confident manner. He kept as much cash on hand as possible. When investors and creditors would come around he would let them know in one way or another, the amount of cash he had. He didn't bother to tell them that practically all his assets were in cash. He had his back to the wall more than once, but by acting as if he could not fail — and as if he meant to be a success — he inspired others with his same confidence.

John D. Rockefeller used the same technique. When a creditor came calling and subtly suggested he would like to have his bill paid, Rockefeller would reach for his checkbook with a flourish. "Which would you rather have," he would ask, "cash or Standard Oil stock?" He appeared so calm and confident that nearly all decided to take stock in his company, and none ever lived to regret it.

### Money in the bank for salesmen

Bob Whitney, president of National Sales Executives, New York City, told me recently, "Les, a confident manner in a salesman is like having money in the bank. Act confident. Look confident. And you'll find that you begin to feel more confident. More important, your prospects will begin to have more confidence in you. I've seen mediocre salesmen make a good record because they knew how to act and talk in a confident manner. And I've seen men who apparently knew all the answers about theoretical salesmanship fail miserably because they did not have this knack of displaying the confident manner."

### How to put magnetism in your personality

Bob Bale, founder of the famous Bob Bale Personality Institute, tells me that this same feeling of confidence and the adoption of a confident manner is one of the most important things you can do to make yourself a more interesting, dynamic personality.

"No one likes a wishy-washy, namby-pamby sort of person who acts as if he didn't quite know what he was talking about or what he wants," says Bob.

"We instinctively like the person who knows what he wants, and acts as if he expects to get it. People don't like doubters or failures. If you want people to like you let them know that you *expect to win*. Hold up your head. Look the other person in the eye. Walk as if you had somewhere to go and meant to get there. I have seen men and women completely change their personalities by a *deliberate* adoption of the confident manner."

Remember, if you believe in yourself and *act as if you believe in yourself, others will believe in you.*

## Little Things Give You Away

You can't look inside a man's skull and see how much confidence is inside it. But confidence has a way of showing itself in little subtle ways. And while we may never have analyzed just why we have confidence in another person, subconsciously we all judge others by these little "signs" or "clues" that give them away.

### 1. Watch your walk

*Our physical actions express our mental attitudes.* If you see a man walking along with shoulders bent and drooped, you can know that his burdens are almost too heavy for him to bear. He acts as if he were carrying a heavy weight around with him. (He probably is, in the form of discouragement and despair.) When something is weighting down a man's spirit, it invariably weights down his body. He droops.

See a man walking along with head down and eyes downcast and you know he is feeling pessimistic.

A timid person walks with unsure, hesitant steps, as if he were afraid to let go and really step out confidently.

The man with a feeling of confidence steps out boldly. His shoulders are back, and his eyes are looking out and up to some goal he feels he can attain.

## 2. Your tattle-tale handshake

Writing for *Your Life* magazine, John D. Murphy, in an article called "Your Tattle-tale Handshake," says that the way you shake hands tells the other person far more than you suspect about the way you feel about yourself. The limp, dish-rag type handshaker is low on self-confidence. If he tries to act arrogant and powerful, as many people do who are low on self-confidence, you know he is bluffing. The bone-crusher is apt to be compensating for a lack of self-confidence. He goes to too great an extreme to impress you that he really is confident. The firm, but not crushing handshake, with just a little squeeze in it that says, "I'm alive. I've got a firm grasp of things," is the handshake that denotes self-confidence.

## 3. Your tone of voice

Actually we express ourselves through our voices more than in any other way. The voice is the most highly developed means of communication between human beings. But your voice communicates more than ideas. It also communicates your feelings about yourself. Begin to listen to your own voice. Does it express hopelessness or courage? Have you, without realizing it, gotten into the habit of talking in a whining way? Do you speak up confidently—or mumble?

### How to Use the Only Way to Make People Do Better

Many people try to make others do better by scolding, shaming, threatening, or giving advice on what they "ought" to do. The trouble is that these methods just do not work. Most often they make matters worse. Obeying a basic law of human nature to "live up to" the opinions of others and to act out appropriately the part he is given, the accused and blamed person will do what seems to be expected of him, will try to fulfill your view of him. Your scolding and disapproval only convince the other person that you are disappointed in him, that you have a low opinion of him, and again you will see your own opinions reflected back to you in the other person's actions.

Winston Churchill, who is truly a master in the art of dealing with people, once said, "I have found that the best way to get another to *acquire* a virtue, is to *impute* it to him."

Let the other fellow know you think he *can* be trusted and he will prove himself trustworthy.

In the little town of Sunset, Louisiana, there is a banker by the name of Robert J. Castile, head of the Bank of Sunset and Trust Company, who has made hundreds of loans without collateral or co-signers. He even loans money to high school graduates, who are minors, without the signature of their parents. He has financed more than 300 college educations for needy students.

Out of more than half-a-million dollars so loaned during the past 15 years, the bank has not lost one cent. The magic is simply that the borrowers are made to know that they are getting the money for one reason and one reason only: the bank expects them to repay, and the bank has faith in them to repay. In 1945, the bank loaned $2,000 to an unemployed man who had no assets whatever, not even a place to live for his family. Every penny was paid back within four years.

*A truth serum that really works.* A law enforcement officer told me recently that the best way he had ever found to get information from shady characters was simply to tell them, "Well, people tell me that you have quite a reputation as a tough guy and that you've been in lots of trouble, but that there is just one thing you won't do and that is to lie. They say that if you tell me anything at all it will be the truth, and that's the reason I'm here."

By imputing the virtue of truthfulness to a hoodlum, this cop literally makes him tell the truth.

When Herbert Hoover was head of price regulation during World War I, word reached him that a certain Midwestern merchant was violating price regulations flagrantly and openly. Hoover decided to try a bit of strategy. He sent the merchant a telegram that said in effect: "You have been appointed Chairman of a Committee on Compliance in your city." The telegram went on to advise that this merchant's cooperation in seeing that the merchants of his city abided by the regulations on a voluntary basis would be greatly appreciated. The telegram worked like magic. Not only did the merchant abide strictly by the regulations from that time on, but he spent a lot of time and effort convincing other merchants to comply. Hoover had used an old trick that school teachers frequently employ when they pick out the most rowdy boy in the class and say, "Jimmy, I am going to have to leave the room for a few minutes and I want you to act as monitor and keep order until I return."

Long ago Emerson said, "Trust men and they will be true to you."

Try it. You'll find that it is not just a platitude, but that it works.

We are not the same person to every person we meet. No man, woman, or child is wholly good or wholly bad. We all have different sides to our personality. Nearly always, the side that we present, is the side that the other fellow brings out in us. It doesn't pay to pre-judge people and decide that so-and-so is a crotchety old skinflint, just because someone you know had that experience with him. Your friend might have brought out the crotchety side of the other fellow. By using common-sense and psychology you may be able to bring out a good and generous side. Anyway, it's worth a try.


### CHAPTER 4 IN BRIEF

1. Whether you realize it or not, you control the actions and attitudes of others by your own actions and attitudes.
2. Your own attitudes are reflected back to you from the other person almost as if you stood before a mirror.
3. Act or feel hostile and the other fellow reflects this hostility back to you. Shout at him, and he is almost

compelled to shout back. Act calmly and unemotion-
ally, and you turn away his anger before it gets started.

4. Act enthusiastic and you arouse the enthusiasm of the
other person.

5. Act confidently and the other person has confidence in
you.

6. Begin today deliberately to cultivate an enthusiastic
attitude. Take a tip from Frank Bettger and act *as
if* you were enthusiastic. Soon you'll feel enthusiastic.

7. Right now, begin deliberately to cultivate a confident
manner. Don't mumble your words as if you were
afraid to express them. Speak out. Watch your pos-
ture. A slumped figure signifies that you find the
burdens of life too heavy for you to bear. A drooping
head signifies that you are defeated by life. Hold your
head up. Straighten up your shoulders. Walk with
a confident step, as if you had somewhere important to
go.

# Chapter 5

# HOW YOU CAN CREATE A GOOD FIRST
# IMPRESSION ON OTHER PEOPLE

A MUSICIAN CAN OFTEN LISTEN TO THE VERY *first* note of a piece of music and tell you in what key the composition is written. In most cases a composition will begin on the same note as the key. If the piece is written in B flat, for example, the first main chord will be B flat. You will also find that most musical compositions *end* on the same keynote.

What has all this to do with human relations? Quite a lot.

The manner in which we approach the other fellow, our very first words and actions, nearly always sound the "keynote" for the entire interview. If you begin by clowning around with a person, it is very difficult to move the interview into a different key. He just won't take you seriously.

*Everybody in the world is literally waiting for you to tell them what to do.* You can control the actions and attitudes of the other person to a remarkable extent if you will remember to start the conversation with him on the same keynote that you want it to end on. If you want him to take you seriously, sound that keynote in your very first words. If you want it to be businesslike, start off in a business-like tone. If you want it to be informal, start off in an informal tone.

Remember, the other person will "rise to the occasion." He will act out his role on the stage setting that *you* provide. Unless you want to be on the defensive during the entire interview — do not begin with an apologetic attitude. A door-to-door sales-

47

man knocks on a door and when the housewife answers, says, "I hate to bother you, Ma'am," or "I won't take up much of your time," and without realizing it he is controlling the attitude of the housewife. He is setting a stage where she can only act out the role of a person who is being bothered and whose time is being taken up.

Caspar Milquetoast goes to a swanky restaurant and says apologetically to the headwaiter, "I'm sorry, but I don't have reservations. I don't suppose I could have a place near the floor show." Without realizing it, he is setting the stage for the head-waiter to act upon. "You certainly *can't* expect to have a center table if you don't bother to get reservations," says the headwaiter, and puts him off in a corner.

You have heard on the radio or television or in the movies the words "lights, camera, action." When these words are spoken, action begins. Cameras start turning, the actors start acting. But the actors aren't just acting willy-nilly. They are acting out roles that have been assigned them. They are acting in accord-ance with a pre-arranged mood. And the "scene" they act out is the scene that fits the stage setting.

Whether you realize it or not, every time you have dealings with another person, you are setting a stage. If you set the stage for comedy, you shouldn't expect him to act out serious drama. If you set the stage for tragedy, don't expect the other person to be gay about it.

Remember that your very first words, actions, and attitudes invariably sound the keynote. Have you ever heard someone say, "We just couldn't seem to get together. Somehow we just got off on the wrong foot"? "It just didn't come off," we say of a meeting or interview that didn't go as we would have liked. Nearly always, when this happens, it is because we got off in the wrong key. We sounded a minor opening chord, and then wondered why the music that followed was so sad.

### *Know what you want, then sound off accordingly*

Dr. Ruth Barbee, director of The Family Relations Institute, Atlanta, Georgia, has helped many husbands and wives patch up their differences. But the one big difficulty, she tells me, is getting them together in her office on a keynote of reconciliation.

"I'll go back to him," says the wife, "If he shows he is sincere."

"I'd be happy to have her come home," says the husband, "only she's got to make the first move."

Getting them together while in this mood is useless, says Dr. Barbee, for one or the other will sound off in a keynote of hostility, and the meeting will invariably end in just another argument. But if one or the other, or better, both, will begin with a keynote that says, "I want you back," almost any difficulty can be overcome.

Before you go into any kind of discussion, it is well to ask yourself the question: "What do I really want from this? How do I want this to go? What mood do I want to prevail?" Then sound off a key-note that will set the stage for that.

### How to Create a Good First Impression

Another way we can control the actions and attitudes of others is to remember that the very first impression we give them is apt to be the lasting impression they have of us. That first meeting usually sounds the keynote. From then on, it is mighty hard to get the other fellow to change his opinion of you.

The other day I was talking with a friend about a certain merchant we both knew. "I don't like him," she said. "He is mean and ill-tempered and treats his wife terribly."

I was flabbergasted.

"I don't understand," I said. "To me he is one of the most pleasant, good-natured fellows in town. And I happen to know that he and his wife are very happy together."

"Well," responded my friend, "all I know is that the first time I ever saw him I walked into his store and he was talking just awful to his wife. He was angry and shouting and just acting terribly."

"Perhaps he did lose his temper one time," I replied. "But that is certainly not typical of him. All of us lose our tempers occasionally, but I'm sure in his case that was the exception rather than the rule."

"I can't help it," she said. "I don't like men who talk to their wives that way, and no matter how nice he is for the rest of his life, I could never like him."

Actually, the merchant in question is one of the most devoted husbands I have ever known. In fact, I don't believe I've ever known a man who was any more thoughtful of his wife — or whose wife was any happier. But, unfortunately, the *first time* my friend saw him, he set the keynote as a mean, overbearing husband, and that is what he will always be to her.

### *Other people accept you at your own appraisal*

You yourself are more responsible for how you are accepted than anyone else. Many people worry about what other people will think of them. But few realize that the world forms its opinion of us, largely from the opinion we have of ourselves. This too, is based on a law of psychology that is as certain as the law of gravitation.

Emerson once said, "It is a maxim worthy of all acceptation that a man may have that allowance he takes. Take the place and attitude which belong to you, and all men acquiesce. The world must be just. It leaves to every man, with profound unconcern, to set his own rate. Hero or driveller, it meddles not in the matter. It will certainly accept your own measure of your doing and being, whether you sneak about and deny your own name, or whether you see your work produced to the concave sphere of the heavens, one with the revolution of the stars."

If you aren't accepted as you would like to be, maybe you should blame yourself. Act as if you were a nobody, and the world will take you at your own value. Act as if you were a somebody, and the world has no choice but to treat you as somebody.

One word of warning is needed here. Many people think they are showing the world what a high opinion they have of themselves when they are arrogant, overbearing, rude and "stuck-up." Actually, they are showing just the opposite.

Remember, the man who *really* has a good opinion of himself does not go to ridiculous lengths to convince himself he is somebody. People who put on airs and try to act what they (wrongly) think is a big-shot role do so because they feel a need to act big. And the reason they feel a need to act big is because they really feel small and insignificant. They are constantly trying to prove to themselves that they are really bigger than they feel.

Really "big" people never act like this. Rather, they are natural and homey. Subconsciously, we are all smarter than we realize. Our conscious mind may not be smart enough to analyze and see through the disguises people wear. But our subconscious does. And our subconscious tells us that the person putting on a big act doesn't really think well of himself at all but is just a phoney.

For example, I know a certain man who goes to great lengths to get his picture in the newspapers. And when he does, he has hundreds of copies made and sends them to everyone he knows. The other day a friend and I were talking about this fellow, who had just sent my friend another cut of himself from some Midwestern newspaper.

"You know," he said, "I'm beginning to wonder. Is he trying to convince me he is a big-shot, or is he really trying to convince himself?"

### How many people unwittingly create a bad impression

People judge you not only by the value you put on yourself. . . they judge you by the value you put on other things: your job, your work, even your competition.

There is a verse in the Bible that says, "Judge not that ye be not judged." It is a good text for human relations. For everytime we judge something, we give other people a clue to judging us.

An attorney who handles many divorce cases said to me, "Often when a husband or wife begins to tell me all the mean, unpleasant things the other partner has done, I learn more about the person who is doing the talking than I learn about the person being talked about."

Negative talk and negative opinions give a bad impression.

Walter Lowen, head of the Walter A. Lowen Placement Agency, New York City, has an impressive record for finding men and women jobs in the upper brackets. It is everyday business for Lowen to place a man in a job paying $50,000 or more per year, and he has been doing this for more than 30 years.

One of the things that he tells each applicant is never to express resentment against his present employer, when being interviewed by a new one. The temptation is to ingratiate yourself with the new man by running down your present boss. There is also a temptation to tell how unjustly you have been treated. Don't do it, says Lowen. "Remember, nobody wants to hire a sorehead."

Ever notice how restless you get when you are forced into the company of a chronic complainer? Ever notice how unpopular the fellow is who is "agin" everything?

What value do you place on your job, on the company you work for? When someone asks you where you work, do you answer half-apologetically, "Oh, I work at the ——— bank," as if you were ashamed of the fact, or do you say proudly, "I work at the best bank in this part of the country." The other person will think more of *you* if you give the second answer.

When someone asks where you're from, do you say, self-consciously — "Oh, it's just a little wide place in the road," or do you say, "I'm from Pleasantville, the greatest little town in the world"?

If you give the impression that your employer isn't much, or anything else you are doing isn't much, then the listener will think that you can't be much yourself or you wouldn't be associated with such a place or doing what you're doing.

*Don't knock the competition.* It is surprising how many salesmen have never learned that people do not like knockers — even people who knock competition. Never knock the other fellow or the other fellow's product if you want to make a good impression. Instead, boost your own product. Not only do people dislike negative talk — and knocking is certainly negative — but also, you set a negative stage. You set the stage for a negative mood — and then wonder why you can't get the prospect to say yes. Besides this, the subconscious mind of the other fellow is smart enough to reason out, "The competition must really be something, or this fellow wouldn't be so afraid of it and go to such lengths to knock it."

## Getting people to say yes to you

Don't expect a "yes" response from the other fellow, if you set a negative stage. The well-known psychologist, Harry Overstreet, in his book *Influencing Human Behavior\**, says that the best way ever discovered by psychology to get a "yes" response is to put the other fellow in a "yes" mood. You do this by creating a positive and affirmative atmosphere, rather than a negative one.

One good rule is to get the other fellow to say "Yes" to a number of preliminary questions. "Isn't this a beautiful color?" or "Don't you agree this is fine workmanship?" After the other person has answered "Yes" five or six times to these preliminary questions, it is much easier for him to say "Yes" to your big question.

*"Yes" can sometimes be negative.* Don't, however, make the mistake of one fellow I know, in trying to carry out this advice. He was such a pessimistic, negative thinker, that even though he asked questions which got a "yes" answer, they were all pitched to create a negative rather than an affirmative mood.

"Isn't the heat terrible today?" he would ask a prospect, and the prospect would say "Yes." "The world is sure in a mess, isn't it?" he'd ask, and again get a "Yes" answer. "With world conditions what they are you never know what to depend on," he'd say.

"Yes, that's right," the prospect would answer. Although he got "Yes" answers, he created a *negative mood.* The prospect was so gloomy and depressed and in such a negative frame of mind that he was in no mood to buy anything.

Pessimistic, gloomy, negative people don't buy goods, and they don't buy ideas. They become cautious and hesitant. Cheerful, optimistic, positive-thinking people are the ones who buy goods or ideas. They are more generous, more willing to expand, more willing to take a chance.

---

\* New York: W. W. Norton and Co., 1925.

*Your question often sets the stage for the answer.* Another rule to employ in getting a "Yes" anwer is to ask a question where the answer is implied in the question. Instead of saying, "Do you like this?", say, "I believe you like this one, don't you?" Instead of saying, "Do you like this color?", say, "This certainly is a beautiful color, isn't it?" or "Isn't this a beautiful color?"

The third rule for helping people say "Yes" is to nod your head affirmatively as you ask the question. Remember, your actions influence the actions of the other person.

### Assume that the other person will do what you want

Dr. Albert Edward Wiggam, whom we have quoted earlier, says, "Hardly anything is stronger in suggestion than the calm assumption that the other fellow is going to do what you want him to do."

One of the most successful men I know of in getting people to do things — and do them gladly — is Dr. Pierce P. Brooks, president of National Banker's Life Insurance Company, Dallas, Texas.

When Dr. Brooks was Chairman of the Board of Stewards of Tyler Street Methodist Church in Dallas, Sunday School attendance increased to such an extent that it set new records for Methodist churches all over the world. Such an achievement requires the efforts and cooperation of many people working together. When he was president of The Texas Safety Council, Dallas set new safety records and became known as the safest city in the U. S. When he organized the Crippled Children's Foundation of America, he not only gave much of his own money, but succeeded in getting many other businessmen to give — one of whom donated the entire profits of one of his companies to the cause. His ability to organize and get people to do things has not only made him a success, but has made him much in demand as a leader of civic and fraternal causes.

When I asked Dr. Brooks the secret of getting people to do things, he said, "I seldom, if ever, ask anyone *if* he will do something. I always try to find some *personal reason* why the other fellow would want to do, then just assume that he does want to do it, and is going to do it. I let them know that *I believe they can do it,* that I have confidence in their ability, that I trust them to do a good job — then leave them alone and let them do it. Constantly looking over a man's shoulder implies that you do not quite trust him to do a good job. I assume that he is going to do a good job, and I'm very seldom disappointed."

In his book, *How Power Selling Brought Me Success in Six Hours,** Dr. Brooks goes on to tell how he uses this technique of calmly assuming that the other person is going to buy, as one of the best methods of closing sales.

Here again, we have the strong urge of a human being to "live up to" what is expected of him.

*If you're not looking for trouble, why ask for it?* Try using this technique on your children. Stop using words that show that you *expect* to be disobeyed, or to get an argument.

For example, if you want your children to go to bed without a lot of resistance, don't say, "Jimmy, dear, it's getting late, and Mommy wishes you would go on and get ready for bed." If you want him to come into the house and rest, don't say, "Oh, I wish I could get you to come in and rest a little, I don't see why you want to keep running around in the hot sun." These statements assume that you expect Jimmy to put up an argument. They assume that he *doesn't* want to go to bed — or come in the house and rest.

Instead, try this: go turn down his covers. Get his pajamas and bring them to him. Kiss him goodnight and say, "Okay, Jimmy, time to go to bed now." If you want him to rest for 30 minutes a day, try setting an alarm clock to go off when the rest period is to begin. When the clock sounds off, go to the door, open it for him, and say simply, "Okay, Jimmy, you can finish that later — it's time for rest period now."

Don't expect these methods to work perfectly, especially if you have educated Jimmy for a long time to the idea that you expect him to argue and show resistance. But these methods will work better than pleading or scolding, and are much easier on your nerves.

When a famous newspaper reporter called at the editorial offices of the *Christian Science Monitor,* he looked around and

---

* Englewood Cliffs, N. J.: Prentice-Hall, Inc., 1955.

did not see any "No Smoking" signs. So he asked, "Is there a rule against smoking in here?"

"No," said the editor "There is no rule. *But nobody ever has.*"

Although the reporter was a chain-smoker, and he was told there was no rule against it — he found he simply *could not smoke,* so strong was the influence of knowing he was not expected to smoke.

### *CHAPTER 5 IN A FEW WORDS*

1. In dealing with other people, you yourself sound the keynote for the entire theme, when you begin the interview.
2. If you start off on a note of formality, the meeting will be formal. Start off on a note of friendliness and the meeting will be friendly. Set the stage for a business-like discussion, and it will be business-like. Start on a note of apology and the other person will force you to play that theme all the way through.
3. When you meet someone for the first time, the impression you make then is very likely to be the keynote that will determine how he regards you for the rest of your life.
4. Other people tend to accept you at your own evaluation. If you think you are a nobody, you are practically asking other people to snub you.
5. One of the best means ever discovered for impressing the other fellow favorably is not to strive too hard to make an impression, but to let him know that he is making a good impression on you.
6. People judge you not only by the opinion you hold of yourself, but also by the opinions you hold on other things: your job, your company, even your competition.
7. Negative opinions create a negative atmosphere. Don't be a knocker. And don't be a sorehead.
8. The way, itself, in which you ask things, sets the stage or sounds the keynote for the other person's answer. Don't ask "no" questions if you want "yes" answers. Don't ask questions or issue instructions that imply you expect trouble. Why ask for trouble?

## Part Three

## TECHNIQUES FOR MAKING AND
## KEEPING FRIENDS

---

# Chapter 6

# HOW TO USE THREE BIG SECRETS FOR ATTRACTING PEOPLE

---

W<small>HAT</small> <small>IS</small> <small>THE</small> <small>SECRET</small> <small>OF</small> <small>AN</small> <small>ATTRACTIVE</small>
personality? We have all known them, those people who just
seem to attract customers and friends. We say that people are
drawn to such a personality, or "he just draws people to him."
Such phrases are very descriptive, for you can't force people
to like you, but you can *draw* them to you if you supply food to
feed three basic human hungers.

Put out a T-bone steak on your back door step and you don't
have to ride herd on the dogs in your neighborhood to get them
to come. They'll be there. And when word gets around that you
have in stock the three basic foods that I want to tell you about
in this chapter, people will be attracted to you in the same way.

*The genuinely "nice guy" whom everybody avoids.* Friendship doesn't just happen. We *choose* our friends. And either
consciously or unconsciously, we choose them on the basis of
need and hunger. Sam Sweettalk may be the nicest, sweetest,
most considerate man you have ever met in your whole life, yet
you may not choose Sam for a personal friend for the simple reason that Sam does not offer any food to feed your hungers. In
fact, you may find yourself uncomfortable in Sam's presence.
All the goodness that is oozing out of him all the time may only
make you feel guilty and inferior. So although Sam is a nice
guy, you avoid him like the plague.

## The Triple-A Formula for Attracting People

Here are three basic hungers that all normal human beings have. You might call this the "Triple-A" Technique for winning friends. For when you use these three "A's," with an understanding of what is behind them, you'll find more and more people automatically warming up to you.

### 1. Acceptance

Acceptance is a vitamin. We all hunger to be accepted *as we are*. We want someone we can relax with. Someone we can let our hair down and take our shoes off with. Very few of us are brave enough to "be ourselves" completely when dealing with the world in general. But we like to have *somebody* that we can be ourselves with, someone we can *afford* to be ourselves with, because we know we will be accepted.

The critical, fault-finding type of person, who always sees where others fall short and can usually also suggest a remedy, is never going to be stampeded by crowds rushing to be his close friends.

Don't set up rigid personal standards of how you think other people ought to act. Give the other person the right to be himself. If he's a little peculiar, let him be. Don't insist that he do everything you do and like everything you like. Let him relax when he is around you.

Strangely enough, the people who accept people, and like them just as they are, have the most influence in changing the other person's behavior for the better. Many a married man who has changed from a wild and wooly character into a solid citizen will tell you (if you can get him to talk about it) that the one thing which enabled him to change was "The faith my wife had in me," or that, "My wife just believed in me. She never criticized or nagged, but just kept on believing in me. Somehow I just had to change."

As one psychologist expressed it, "No one has the power to reform another person, but by liking the other person as he is, you give him the power to change himself."

Many good people have little or no influence on others who

might be influenced by them for the better, simply because they cannot accord the other person any acceptance as he is, but give the other person the idea that he must change someway in order to earn their acceptance.

There is no record that any Pharisee ever changed the con-duct of any sinner. The Pharisees were good people. But their very goodness separated them from other men. They were horrified when Jesus ate with "Publicans and Sinners." They were aghast when he told the woman taken in adultery, "Neither do I condemn thee." But the fact remains that Jesus "had a way with people" that no one had equalled before or has since.

*How psychoanalysts help people do better.* Have you ever considered what really happens when a person is psychoanalyzed? I'm not talking about the movie versions, but a real-life case, where a person with all sorts of fears and problems — a person who can't get along with himself, and can't get along with others — gets "cured," merely by going twice a week to a doctor's office and talking to the doctor.

Recently, I met a prominent psychoanalyst at a dinner party and the talk got around to this matter of acceptance in human relations.

"If people really practiced acceptance, we'd soon be out of business," he told me. "For the very heart of psychoanalysis is that the patient finds one person, the doctor, who will accept him. For the first time in his life, he lets his hair down — he brings out his fears, the things he is ashamed of, and the doctor listens without surprise or horror or moral judgment. Because he has found one human being who shows acceptance in spite of all his 'shameful' traits and faults, he is able to accept himself and then he is on the road to better living."

### How to make your marriage vows come true

Dr. Ruth Barbee says that much marital unhappiness could be avoided if young couples would take to heart those words of the marriage ceremony, "I take this man (or woman) . . . for better or for worse . . ." You must accept the other person *as he is,* she says.

"Emotional acceptance does not mean lowering your ideals," she continues. "It is the way you feel about a person, not the way you think about him. It is an affirmation of him as a person. It is a recognition that basically and fundamentally he is something you can accept. It has to do with the stuff he is made of, rather than what he does or doesn't do."

Everyone needs this feeling of acceptance. No man is accepted by everybody and it is foolish to attempt to be. *But each of us must be accepted by the people who count to us.* The punishment that "The Man Without a Country" suffered was the punishment of being accepted by no one at all. Even the most ruthless of men, who have set themselves against the whole world, feel the need of this acceptance. Hitler, for instance, surrounded himself with a small group of admirers and took them with him everywhere he went.

### Acceptance is a two-edged sword

One of the tragedies of our society is that this need for acceptance works against society as well as for it. The many teen-age gangs that are springing up around the country, for example, are no doubt due in large part to the fact that these boys, who are not accepted in other places in society, do attain some personal significance, some sense of belonging, through the acceptance of the members of the gang.

Another tragedy is that very often when a man gets out of prison, he may have learned his lesson and have only the best of intentions. But he soon finds that an ex-jailbird is not accepted among "nice people." About the only place where he can get a feeling of acceptance is among criminals and other ex-criminals.

### How to make your husband successful

Many big businessmen tell me that before they promote a man they like to find out something about his wife. They are interested not so much in whether she is good-looking and charming, or a good cook, but primarily in whether she gives her husband a feeling of confidence.

The president of one corporation expressed it this way, "When a wife accepts her husband and gives him the feeling that she is pleased with him, as is, it is like getting a shot of self-confidence in the arm everytime the husband goes home. He says to himself, 'if she likes me, maybe I'm not such a bad guy after all.' If she seems to like him and believe in him, he says, 'maybe I can do it after all,' and he goes out to meet the world the next morning brimming over with self-confidence and with the feeling that whatever comes along, he can lick it.

"But when a man goes home to a nagging, complaining, scold-ing wife, it's like having all the fight taken out of him. Her continual dissatisfaction with him comes across to him and adds to his germ of self-doubt. He begins to doubt himself."

He might have added that a wife who gives her husband acceptance not only gives him a dose of self-confidence, but also gives him a good dose of human-kindness, and that easy-to-get-along-with quality. For, by her acceptance, she helps him to like himself better. When he likes himself better, he is going to be easier to get along with. He is going to be more thoughtful and considerate. The wife who is continually nagging, on the other hand, gets just the opposite of what she wants. She helps her husband like himself less. And the lower his self-esteem sinks, the more irritable and fault-finding he is going to be with her. Perhaps it is poetic justice, after all.

Of course, everything I've said about wives applies just as much, if not more so, to husbands. Men can be greater naggers than women, and the sarcastic, fault-finding, ego-deflating hus-band also gets what he asks for.

## 2. *Approval*

The second magic "A" that everyone hungers for is *approval*.

Approval goes a little further than acceptance. Acceptance is mostly negative in comparison. We accept the other person with his faults and short-comings and still accord him our friendship. But approval means something more positive. It goes beyond just tolerating another's faults, and finds something positive that we can *like*.

You can always find something to approve of in the other person — and you can always find something to disapprove of. It depends upon what you're looking for. If you are a negative type personality you are always looking for flaws, always on the lookout for things you can disapprove of. If you're a positive type personality, you're on the lookout for things you can approve of.

Negative personalities literally bring out the worst in us, for they highlight all the things that are wrong with us. Positive personalities bring out the good in us, by highlighting something they can approve of. We bask in the sunlight of their approval, and the feeling is so good that we start trying to develop other traits and characteristics to draw approval and give us that good feeling all over again.

### A cure for incorrigible children

A child psychologist told me not long ago about a boy who was brought to him labeled "incorrigible." The child was supposed to be "uncontrollable." He was moody, and at first wouldn't even talk to the psychologist. There simply seemed to be no "handle" with which to take hold of him. The psychologist got his clue from a remark made by the boy's father, who said, "This is the only child I've ever seen who doesn't have a single likeable trait, not a single one."

The psychologist started looking for some one thing he could approve. He found several. The boy liked to carve and he did it well. At home he had carved up the furniture and been punished for it. The psychologist bought him a carving set, a set of carving knives, and some soft wood. He also gave him some suggestions about how to use them, and didn't hold back his approval. "You know, Jimmy," he said, "you can carve out things better than any boy I ever knew."

Well, to make a long story short, he soon found other things to approve, and one day Jimmy surprised everyone by cleaning up his own room without being asked. When the psychologist asked him why he did, he said, "I thought you would like that."

## Go out of the way to approve

We are all hungry for approval. And it doesn't have to be a big thing in order to satisfy our hunger. Praise a stock broker about his ability to buy and sell stocks and it has little effect on him. He is apt to think you are merely flattering him, because his success as a stock broker is too obvious. But if you will let him know that you approve of the way he broils a steak over charcoal, he will call your name blessed.

A good rule to remember in complimenting people is this: People are more pleased at a compliment if you praise them for some virtue that is not glaringly obvious. If a man has the physique of a Greek God the chances are that he knows this already, and there is *little doubt* in his mind about it. He doesn't need any confirmation. But he may be good at other things, which are not so obvious. Seek these out and praise him for them, and watch him glow!

## 3. Appreciation is magic

Another basic hunger is the *hunger for appreciation.*

The word *appreciate* really means to *raise in value,* or the opposite of *depreciate,* which means to *lower in value.* We are always looking for people who will raise us in value, rather than lower us in value.

Dr. Pierce P. Brooks told me recently that the success of his insurance companies is due in large part to the motto: "We appreciate our agents." When I asked how such a simple motto could work such a miracle (a leading insurance magazine recently described the growth of his companies as "miraculous") he pointed out the fact that *appreciate* is just the opposite of *depreciate.*

"We *value* our agents highly," he said, "and we let them know we value them highly. We know that the success of any company depends upon the success of its agents. They are important to us. We think they are the best in the business — and all our dealings with them are on that basis. When you appreciate a person, you actually make him more valuable and more suc-cessful."

### *Other people* are *valuable to you*

Stop and consider just how *valuable* other people are to you — your wife, husband, children, your boss, your employees, your customers. Emphasize their value in your own mind. Then figure out little ways to let the other person know you value him highly. And always remember that people *are* the most important, the most valuable things on earth. Here are a few ways to show appreciation. Give it a little thought and you can think of many more:

1. Don't keep people waiting, if you can help it.
2. If you have a caller whom you cannot see immedi-ately—acknowledge his presence and let him know you will see him as soon as possible.
3. Thank people.
4. Treat people as "special."

No. 4 is worth a little additional comment. One of the most deflating, depreciating things in the world to a human being is to be given "the routine treatment." We all want to be treated "special," as an individual — recognized for our own unique worth. If Mary finds out that John "tells that to all the girls," she feels that John has depreciated her. She would much prefer that his theme song be "for you alone.".

Dr. Pierce P. Brooks tells me that he once sent out form letters to prospects in connection with a new subdivision he was opening up. The letter began "Dear friend," and the response was almost zero. By changing those two words, and typing in the addressee's own name, *i. e.*, "Dear Mr. Smith," the return on the mailing was very successful.

*Don't talk station-to-station, but person-to-person*

People don't like to be classified and pigeon-holed into broad general categories such as "customers," "people," "children," "married couples." They want to be acknowledged as one particular and unique "customer" or person.

The skeptic who says, "All customers are just alike" is headed down the road to bankruptcy whether he knows it or not. The woman who says "All men are just alike" is apt to live out the rest of her days in spinsterhood. It is easy to fall into the habit of treating people as "customers," but it doesn't pay. Remember, whatever you're doing — you never deal with "customers" in the abstract. You are always dealing with one individual person. You never learn to get along with "people." You learn to get along with *this* person and *that* person. There is no such animal as "people." The world is populated with individual persons. *People* is just an abstract term.

*We like to be singled out, not considered one of the mob*

We like to go to those restaurants where we are given individual treatment. It doesn't have to be much. Perhaps the head waiter only calls you by name, and says, "Mr. Jones, you'll be happy to know we have shish-kebab tonight."

"We don't usually do this, but in your case I'm going to make an exception," someone says to us. We glow all over.

"Mrs. Smith, I am *personally* going to take care of this matter and see that you get what you want."

"Just anybody couldn't wear this dress, but you can get away with it."

Even children respond to this magic. They don't like to be treated as "children," but as Jimmy Jones, individual. Don't compare him with the kid down the street. This only depreciates him. Many a man, when introducing his family, will single out his wife as an individual person — "This is Mrs. Jones" — and dismiss with a wave of the hand his three children — "and these

are the children." Why depersonalize them? Why not introduce them the same as you would any other individual person?

By the same token, when you're introduced to a teen-ager,
acknowledge the introduction the same as if you were being
introduced to the president of a bank. Instead of just waving
your hand and saying, "Hi," why not shake hands and say,
"Hello, Dick, I'm very happy to meet you."?

### Take a lesson from Mother Nature

Take a lesson from the flowers. They know how to attract
bees. They want the bee to pollinate them. They need the bee.
But instead of pleading or scolding or coercing, the flower just
puts out a few drops of nectar. The flower knows that the bee
is hungry for nectar. It provides food to feed that hunger.

If you will analyze the person with the attractive personality,
you will find that he too, offers food to feed these basic hungers
of human beings.

There is an old saying, in effect, that "honey attracts more
flies than vinegar." It is often interpreted to mean that you
should "sweet-talk" your way to what you want. A closer look,
however, will show that honey attracts flies, simply because
honey is food that the fly wants and needs. Put out a bowl of
honey and you don't have to go up and down the street with
a sound truck telling the flies about it. You don't have to organize committees to convince the flies they should come. They'll
be there.

And when you begin to put out these three basic foods, you
can count on people to flock to you in droves.

### A QUICK RUN-DOWN ON CHAPTER 6

1. The real secret of an *attractive personality* is to offer
   other people the food they are hungry for. People are
   as hungry for certain things as flies are for honey.
2. Use the Triple-A Formula for attracting people:
   Acceptance.  Accept people as they are. Allow
   them to be themselves. Don't insist

|  | on anyone being perfect before you can like him. Don't fashion a moral strait jacket and expect others to wear it in order to gain your acceptance. Above all don't bargain for acceptance. Don't say, in substance, "I'll accept you if you'll do this or that, or change your ways to suit me." |
| --- | --- |
| Approval. | Look for *something* to approve in the other person. It may be something small or insignificant. But let the other person know you approve *that*, and the number of things you can sincerely approve of will begin to grow. When the other person gets a taste of your genuine approval, he will begin to change his behavior so that he will be approved for other things. |
| Appreciation. | To appreciate means to raise in value. as opposed to depreciate, which means to lower in value. Let other people know that you value them. Treat other people as if they were valuable to you. Don't keep them waiting. Thank them. Give them "special", individual treatment. |

# Chapter 7

# HOW TO MAKE THE OTHER FELLOW FEEL
# FRIENDLY – INSTANTLY

---

Have you ever known one of those fellows who "never met a stranger?" He seems to make friends instantly. He sits down next to someone on a bus and right away they are talking away as if they were old friends. He calls upon a prospect, and the prospect starts right off dealing with him as if they had been old friends all their lives.

On the other hand we have all known people who are "nice" — once you get to know them — but are hard to get to know. The first class seem to have some magic — almost as if they can "turn on" a friendly feeling in the other fellow, while the second, "hard-to-get-to-know" type are handicapped in getting along in the world. While they are "warming up" to the other fellow — some "easy-to-know" fellow has already taken the business and gone.

### How to use the magic switch that turns on friendly feelings

I learned about these "easy-to-know" types when I was in college. I was a little on the shy side as far as girls were concerned. If I saw a good looking girl, I would *want* to ask her for a date, but instead would tell myself, "She wouldn't like it if I just went up and asked her for a date. She would probably think I was being too fresh. She probably has a date anyway — probably going steady with the best-looking boy in school and wouldn't even consider going out with me."

So I'd sit back and think about ways that I could get introduced to her, and what I was going to say to her. Sometimes, I'd
get up enough nerve to start a conversation with a girl I didn't
know, and I'd walk up to her and mumble out my little prepared
speech, and nine times out of ten the girl would react just as
I had pictured in my imagination that she would react. She'd
either put on a show of indignation and say, "I don't believe
I know you," or she would appear to be amused by my awkward
manner.

Now with my roommate all this was different. He was one
of those "easy-to-know" types. He'd walk up to a girl he'd never
seen before in his life, start a conversation, and in two minutes
they'd be laughing and talking like old friends. No one ever
called him "fresh." They actually seemed to like his bold
approach.

### How I learned my roommate's secret

Finally, one day I got him to tell me his secret. "You've got
to *believe* the other fellow is going to like you," he said. Well,
with that clue, I got to watching my roommate more closely.
He was as popular with the boys on the campus as he was with
the girls. Everyone seemed to like him. He even worked his
magic on the professors. He could get by with things in class
that I would have been thrown out for. Yet, the professors
would just laugh, and seemed to think he was a fine fellow.
And as I watched him operate, I noticed that he always acted
just as if the other fellow's friendly response was a foregone
conclusion. Because he *believed* other people would like him,
he *acted as if* they would like him. In short,

### He Assumed the Attitude He Expected the Other Person to Take.

Another thing I noticed was this: Because he *was* thoroughly
convinced that the other person would be friendly, he **was not**
afraid of people. He was not on the defensive.

*Fear of people drives them away*

Fear is one of the greatest handicaps to getting to know people quickly and getting off on a friendly footing. You are afraid that the other fellow will not like you—so you hole up in your shell, like a snail that thinks it is about to be attacked. People can't get close to you because you're so far back in your defensive shell. And because our own attitudes are catching, and have an influence on the other fellow, he begins to withdraw also.

Nothing is truer in the field of human relations than this: If your basic attitude is that other people will be unfriendly— or that "people just don't like me"—your experience will prove it to be so. But if you have the basic attitude that "Most people are friendly, and want to be friendly toward me"—again your experience will prove it so.

*Take a chance he's friendly. The odds are in your favor*

Get over your fear that the other person will "snub you." Take the risk. *Bet on his being friendly*. You won't win every time, but the odds are heavily in your favor. Remember that most people do crave friendship, just as you do. It is a universal craving. The reason the other fellow does not always appear friendly may be that he is afraid of *you*, afraid that *you* will reject *him*.

Take the initiative. Don't wait for some token of friendship from the other fellow. Make the first move. And chances are you'll see him begin to warm up.

*Don't be an eager-beaver*

We all know people who are eager-beavers to win the other fellow's approval. They are the folks who "try too hard" to be charming, who knock themselves out to arouse friendly feelings in the other person.

Most of us also know that the eager-beaver is seldom, if ever, popular.

All of us know girls who try so hard to get married that they scare all the men away. Many of these girls have looks, charm, beauty, all the desirable traits—and would have no trouble at all doing the very thing they want so much to do, if they just didn't try so hard.

Many times, the fellow who wants a certain job so badly that "it shows" doesn't get it. Not long ago I was having lunch with two friends and they brought up the name of some fellow they both knew, named "Bill."

"Did Bill ever get that promotion?" said one.

"No, the last report I had, he still hadn't gotten it," said the other.

"What in the world is wrong? He is certainly in line for it. He has the ability and everything else to get it."

"I don't know what the trouble is," was the answer, "unless he is just too anxious for it."

### Relax—and take it for granted that you'll be liked

In any human relations situation, it does not pay to be overly-anxious, to let the other person know you are practically drooling to get what you want.

The other person has a strong natural tendency to balk at any action he feels you are "red-hot" for his doing. His instinct will be to drive a harder bargain or he may become suspicious that things are not as they seem. When you give the impression that you want the action very much, when you show anxiety—you also start him wondering why you are trying so hard, and doubts creep in.

When a person comes begging for friendship—the tendency is to back away from him. This is due not to some perverse trait of human nature—but to the same law of psychology we have been talking about. The eager-beaver is *afraid*—deathly afraid—the other person will not like him, or will not do what he wants. Instead of saying to himself, "I know the other fellow is going to like me," he says to himself, "I am terribly afraid he won't like me." This gets across to the other person. The eager-beaver isn't showing any faith in himself.

The trick is not to knock yourself out trying to make the other fellow come through. Just relax, and *know* that he will be friendly and reasonable. Then you'll be relaxed and calm and collected in dealing with the other fellow. One thing the eager-beaver *can* do is smile. It's almost impossible to be worried and anxious while you're smiling. A smile is relaxing. A smile shows confidence. A smile shows that you "just know" the other fellow is going to come through as expected.

### Work Miracles with a Smile

Another thing I noticed about my college roommate: he was always smiling. He was the smilin'est fellow I ever met. If you think of the easy-to-know people that you know, you will find that without exception they are great smilers. They are cheerful and laugh a lot. A real, sincere smile works almost like a "magic switch" that turns on a friendly feeling in the other fellow instantly.

### What a smile says

A good sincere smile says several things to the other fellow. It says not only "I like you—I come as a friend," but it also says "I assume that you are going to like me." When a little puppy dog comes up to you wagging its tail, it is saying, "I'm confident you're a good guy and that you like me."

Another important thing a smile says is, "You are *worth* smiling at." In her book, *Understanding Fear in Ourselves and Others,** Bonaro Overstreet says, "The person at whom we smile, smiles back. In one sense, he smiles at us. In a deeper sense, his smile reports the sudden well-being we have enabled him to experience. He smiles because our smile has made him feel *smile-deserving*. We have, so to speak, picked him out of the crowd. We have differentiated him and given him individual status."

---

* New York: Harper & Brothers, 1951.

### Smile from way down deep

Voice teachers are always telling their pupils to "breathe deep" and let their voices come from "way down deep."

If you want your smile to be a friend-maker, it, too, must come from way down deep. In this case, not from the diaphragm —but from the heart. A smile that goes no further than the lips is no good. Remember, it is not gimmicks which influence the other person, but your true feelings about them.

The best advice I have ever run across on how to smile is given by Joseph A. Kennedy in his Prentice-Hall, Inc., booklet, "Relax and Sell." "Learn to smile on the inside," he says. "It is your FEELING that gets across to the customer's subconscious—not your facial expression. Consciously trying to smile by mechanically manipulating the muscles of your mouth does more harm than good. Instead, forget about your mouth and smile mentally. Imagine that you feel 'smiley' inside. When you do this you are relaxed, for its is impossible to feel friendly and be tense, or to feel hostile and be relaxed."

### Let go and smile!

One simple reason many of us do not smile more often—or more sincerely—is the habit we have of always holding in our true feelings. We have been taught that it isn't quite nice to show the world our feelings. We try not to wear our hearts on our sleeves, or show our feelings on our faces. Maybe you think you haven't got a "good smile" and could never learn to smile attractively.

However, my experience has been that everyone is blessed with a good smile. This is something everyone has in him. It's just a question of letting it out. It is just a matter of getting over the fear of showing your true feelings, letting go—and the smile will come out by itself. For when you feel friendly, and feel good about the world, you have to "hold in" a smile.

All that is required is a little practice in expressing your feelings. You'll find that the more you practice, the less inhibited you are. I have seen folks who were regular old sourpusses and poker-faces develop an attractive smile, just by daily practice in *letting go*. When you feel friendly, just "let yourself go." Don't be ashamed or self-conscious about letting your face say, "Boy, am I glad to see you!"

### How to use mirror-magic

Try practicing every morning before your bathroom mirror. Remember something pleasant—something you really liked and got a kick out of. Then—just let go and let this feeling break out over your face. Think of all the wonderful things that could happen to you today—see yourself selling everyone you call on, dealing successfully with every person you meet. Conjure up "good feelings"—then let them out.

Think that's a silly thing to do? You don't believe that such a simple thing can make any difference in the way people react to you? Frank Bettger, writing in *Your Life* magazine, tells how he used a *daily morning smile-practice session* virtually to remake his personality within a very short time. Soon, he found people warming up to him quicker—receiving him on more friendly terms. His sales skyrocketed.

### How to develop a genuine smile

If you have trouble conjuring up a "smiley" feeling at first, don't worry about it. Go ahead and go through the motions anyway. Say the word "cheese" to yourself in the mirror. Get your smile muscles warmed up, and you'll begin to feel more optimistic. Our actions determine our feelings just as much as our feelings determine our actions. William James once said that it is impossible to feel pessimistic when you have the corners of your mouth turned up— and impossible to feel optimistic when you have the corners of your mouth turned down.

Charles Darwin, the discoverer of evolution, wrote a little-known scientific book, *Expression of Emotions in Man and Animals,* in which he traced all the scientific reasons why we have certain bodily expressions to go with certain emotions. He, too, came to the conclusion that emotion and expression are so tied together in our habit system that you simply cannot really feel an emotion completely unless you express it.

The very act of smiling helps you feel more friendly. Mirror practice in smiling helps you develop a good, genuine smile, because it forces you to use the right smile muscles and go through the actions of a real smile, instead of a phoney one. People who give you a phoney, superficial smile really aren't smiling at all. They aren't even using the right smile muscles. And if they could see themselves in a mirror they would realize that they are not smiling at all. This is the reason that the people with a phoney smile do not get a genuine feeling of friendliness by going through the motions of smiling. They are going through the motions of a phoney smile, and the only feeling they get is a feeling of being a phoney.

Everyone can recognize a real smile when he sees one. Practice before your mirror until you see a *real smile*. Many people have never learned what a real smile feels like.

### You can test the power of a smile

Recently I gave a talk to the personnel of an outstanding chain of dairy stores throughout Ohio and neighboring states. My talk included some hints on smiling and what magic it could accomplish when rightly used.

Some weeks later I had occasion to meet one of the secretaries of this concern. She was quite enthused and anxious to tell me about some of her wonderful discoveries. After hearing my talk she decided to test my theory on smiling. She selected as her test the shopping tour she was going to make the next day during her lunch hour. The next day turned out to be a very humid day, raining hard and generally disagreeable and depressing. The stores were crowded nevertheless, and she despaired of being able to buy the five items she needed because they were each in different departments in three different stores.

She remembered my suggestion to give the other fellow a big smile, before saying a word. She was able to complete all five transactions in less than the 30 minutes. Never before had she accomplished so much shopping in so short a time. She was really thrilled because she had received the best service and had gotten the finest treatment at all stores. One counter was surrounded by a large group of women, anxious to be waited on. Most of them were scowling and impatient. The young lady caught the eye of the salesclerk and gave her a big smile, and got waited on first!

### Use your million-dollar asset

If you're not using your smile, you're like a man with a million dollars in the bank and no checkbook. A smile is the million-dollar asset in your human relations inventory. From long experience in dealing with people, and in teaching people how to develop their smiles in my Human Relations and Sales Clinics, I've come to the conclusion that everyone has a million-dollar smile locked up inside him.

### What else has the magic of a smile?

What else can perform the magic of a smile?

Pay someone a compliment—and smile—and it multiplies the compliment many times.

Ask someone a favor — and smile — and he feels almost compelled to grant it.

Accept a favor from someone else — and smile — and you add to the appreciation the other fellow feels.

Even when you have to use somewhat "plain talk"—a smile takes the sting out. "Smile when you say that," we say to a friend—and if he smiles, almost anything he says is all right.

Meet someone for the first time — and smile — and he feels like he's known you all his life.

You couldn't buy a magic elixir like that if you had all the money in the world. Yet the Good Lord gave you just such magic. All you have to do is bring it out of hiding, dust it off, and put it to use,

## CHAPTER 7 IN SUMMARY

1. Human relations often become deadlocked because each party is afraid to make the first move.
2. Don't wait for a sign from the other fellow. Assume that he is going to be friendly, and act accordingly.
3. Assume the attitude that you wish the other person to take. Act as if you expected him to like you.
4. Take a chance that the other fellow will be friendly. It is always a gamble, but you'll win 99 times for every time you lose, if you'll just bet on his being friendly. Refuse to take the chance, and you'll lose every time.
5. Don't be an eager-beaver. Don't be overly anxious. Don't knock yourself out trying to make the other fellow like you. Remember, there is such a thing as being too charming and trying too hard.
6. Just relax and take for granted that other people do like you.
7. Use the magic of your smile to warm up the other fellow.
8. Starting today, begin to develop a genuine smile by practicing before your bathroom mirror. You know what a real smile looks like when you see one. Your mirror will tell you whether your smile is real or phoney. Also, going through the motions of smiling will get you in the habit, and actually make you feel more like smiling.

## Part Four

# HOW EFFECTIVE SPEAKING TECHNIQUES CAN HELP YOU TO SUCCEED

---

# Chapter 8

# HOW YOU CAN DEVELOP SKILL IN USING WORDS

IF TALKING TO OTHERS IS ONE OF YOUR WEAK points in human relations, I strongly urge you to read Harry Simmons' interesting and helpful book, *How to Talk Your Way to Success.**

After more than 25 years in business management and human relations work, Mr. Simmons says that he has found that success often depends as much upon your ability or inability to talk as upon your ability to do your job.

When I first heard the title of Simmons' book, it seemed to me somewhat of an exaggeration. But then I got to thinking about the successful men and women I know. As I went on down the list, it turned out that every single one was a good talker.

### The one thing successful people have in common

Wilfred Funk, editorial director of *Your Life* magazine, made a study of thousands of successful men and women, looking for some one common denominator. He found that the one thing that all these people had in common was *skill in using words.* He found earning power and word skill so closely tied together that you can safely expect to increase your earnings simply by increasing your word power.

* (Englewood Cliffs, N. J.: Prentice-Hall, Inc., 1954)

*Happiness depends on talk*

Our happiness, too, depends to a great extent upon our ability
to express our ideas, desires, hopes, ambitions, or disappoint-
ments to other people by the use of talk. Explorers who return
from lonely expeditions will tell you that what they miss most
is the "small talk" with other human beings. Psychiatrists have
found that many people are unhappy because, for one reason
or another, they are unable to express themselves, and carry
their ideas and emotions around bottled up inside them.

*How to "strike up" a conversation*

Many people are handicapped because they do not know how
to start a conversation, especially with a stranger. They have
a wealth of interesting ideas on tap, if they only knew how to
turn them on. But they hold back because it would seem inane
to start off abruptly with some profound observation on the
nature of man or the universe, and they are afraid they will
be thought dull or obvious if they come out with something as
trite as, "Well, it looks as if it might rain."

William James hit the nail on the head when he said that the
reason so many people find it difficult to be good conversationalists is that they are "afraid of either saying something too
trivial and obvious, or something insincere, or something un-
worthy of one's interlocutor, or in some way or other not adequate to the occasion."

His remedy was, "Conversation does flourish and society is
refreshing . . . whenever people take the brakes off their hearts,
and let their tongues wag as automatically and irresponsibly as
they will."

*Stop trying to be perfect.* John D. Murphy, writing in *Your
Life* magazine in an article called, "Stop Trying to Be Perfect,"
said:

"No one can scintillate every minute. We do not squeeze
bon mots and literary gems out of the brain by taking thought.
They come out unexpectedly and spontaneously, when we relax

and stop being afraid to be ourselves. . . . Ruskin once said that he wrote well only when he was not trying to write well. Henry James the Elder once wrote a friend, 'People often ask me "what do you think?" How do I know what I think until I open my mouth and speak it?'

"Most of us have an entirely false mental picture of what is expected of us. Shakespeare was not afraid to be trite. Choose any classic . . . and you will discover long passages of outright dullness. . . .

"Lask week I made some notes of conversational answers given by three of the most popular emcees on television. Here are a few actual samples: 'No, really?' 'You don't say.' 'Well, now! That is something.' 'Well, what do you know about that.'

"In even the most stimulating conversations fully 50 per cent of what is said is not only trite but absolutely meaningless . . . at least in the early stages. After a 'warm-up' period when the mental wheels are turning easily, the entire conversation can become original—provided the participants are not too much concerned with making it so. It is somewhat like mining for gold. No prospector in his right mind would reject ore—or feel ashamed of it—that did not assay 24 carat gold. Unless you are willing to take a lot of worthless rock and earth, along with a small amount of gold at the beginning, you will never dig down where the vein is richer."

*Small talk isn't supposed to be brilliant.* Everyone is trite. Everyone engages in "small talk" that doesn't say anything clever or significant. This sort of small talk is necessary to get the wheels turning. Once you realize this, and stop being afraid of being dull, you will find that you too can start a conversation, even with a perfect stranger, and you may be surprised to find that in many cases, you *are* saying clever and interesting things —only because you aren't trying to.

*How to warm up to your subject.* Be willing to go through a "warm-up" period in starting conversation. Don't expect to be "hot" at the very beginning. Listen to the experts on television. They know that small talk not only can start a conversation for *them,* but that it can be used to warm up and unlimber the other person. They don't try to draw out any interesting ideas from the other person until they have him warmed up: "Well, and what is your name? Where are you from? What does your husband do? How many children have you? How long are you going to be here? What brings you to New York?"

Who cares?, you may ask. Certainly there is nothing brilliant or clever in these questions. Yet they do get the conversation rolling, and they tend to draw out the other person.

*How to bring out interesting talk from others.* Listen to the answers these experts give. When the guest says she is from Sioux City, he says, "From Sioux City!" When she says she is married and has five children, he says, "Five children! Well, what do you know."

These men are not dull or dumb. But they go on in this vein, giving perfectly inane and trite answers and comments while both they and the other person warm up to each other. Soon they are bringing out interesting facts, clever remarks, funny incidents.

Now, if these experts, who are paid thousands of dollars a week because of their ability as conversationalists, cannot start right in with a bang, what makes you think you can? If they are not afraid to be trite and obvious, why should you be?

*Get him talking about himself.* The next time you are introduced to someone and "cannot think of a thing to say," take a lesson from these TV and radio experts. Try warming up the other fellow with such questions as these:

"Where are you from, Mr. Jones?"

"How long do you plan on being in our city?"

"What do you think of our weather?"

"Do you have a family?"

"What business are you in?"

There are surefire warmer-uppers because they get the other fellow talking about himself. They break the ice and thaw out the other fellow, because they show that you are interested in him. You do not have to look for a topic he can talk about. You start him right off on the *one topic* that he is an expert on —*himself.*

The words *strike up* a conversation are significant. You "strike up" a conversation just as you "strike up" a bonfire. You do not expect to start right off with a raging fire. You strike only one little match, to begin with. The fact that we speak of "breaking the ice," "thawing out" the other fellow, and so on, shows that we already subconsciously recognize the fact that good con versations require a "warm-up" period.

*How to break the ice with strangers.* You'll find you can us this same method to start conversations with strangers on plane busses, and trains. You'll make your trip more pleasant and ma very well meet someone who'll turn into a permanent friend Don't try to think up something profound or clever to say. Just make some observation, or ask some question. Comment on what is happening around you.

"Well, it looks like we are about to get under way at last."

"Boy, it's hot in here; wish those people up front would open the windows."

Another good method is to ask questions. Asking him for information not only warms the other fellow up and gives him an opening, but makes the other fellow feel good because he is in a position to do you a small favor.

"Can you tell me what time it is?"

"What time does this plane get to Kansas City?"

"Does the Riverside bus come by here?"

Simple? Easy? Sure it is. This is the way that conversations get started. The reason most people cannot get started talking is that they try too hard, and try to make something difficult out of it.

### U-turns and green lights keep conversation going

The art of being a good conversationalist consists not so much in thinking up a lot of clever things to say, or heroic experiences you can relate, but in opening up the other fellow and getting him to talk.

If you can stimulate other people to talk—you will acquire a reputation as a good conversationalist. Moreover, if you can get the other fellow talking, and keep him talking, nothing will work better to get him to warm up to *you,* and be more interested in and receptive to *your ideas,* when you are talking.

A friend told me recently of trying several times, unsuccessfully, to get out on a fishing pier in order to get a good view of boat races that were being held in the bay. Each time a city policeman stopped him. "There are too many people out there already," the cop would say, "and I can't let anyone else on the pier until some of those people leave."

"There were four of us in my party," my friend said, "including a woman who had quite a reputation as a talker. When I was turned down the third time, she said, 'let me try.' She went out and talked with the cop for about five minutes, then motioned for us to come on out and he let us go by. When I asked her what in the world she said to him, she told me, 'Oh, I didn't ask him if we could go out on the pier—I just got to talking to him. I asked him whether he didn't get terribly hot having to stand out there in the sun, and said that he must have quite a trying job policing such a mob of people. He told me about how he liked to fish and so forth, and then I just said that we were down here and especially wanted to see the races, but were very disappointed because we couldn't see anything back there on the sea wall. Then he spoke up and said, "Why don't you go on out on the pier, you can see good from there." ' "

*You is a magic word.* This story illustrates very well one of the secrets of making conversation serve you. It can be expressed thus: "Give your conversation a U-turn, and the other fellow will give you a Green Light."

Making a "U-turn" may not be the thing to do in traffic, but in conversation it is a must. *You* is a magic word if you use it correctly. Most of us tend to turn the conversation around to *I* and *Me*. When we do this the other person is apt to give us a red light. This is what happened to my friend who tried to get past the cop on the pier. He just walked out and talked about "I" and "me." "I would like to go out on the pier." "Will you let me get out there?"

The cop gave him a red light and stopped him in his tracks. It is doubtful that the cop even heard everything he said; he probably turned on a red light in his mind and shut him out.

On the other hand, when the lady went out and began to talk about the policeman—emphasizing "You" in the conversation—

she got him warmed up and friendly, and he not only gave her a green light, but actually invited her to go on out on the pier.

Remember what has been said in earlier chapters in this book about human beings being interested first, last, and always in themselves. Apply this knowledge, by realizing that "U" is a go-ahead signal in conversation, while "I" is a stop sign.

*How to ask questions to interest others.* Keep the conversation steered to the other fellow's interest by asking questions: Why? Where? How?

When he says, "I've got a little 25-acre place back home in Indiana," don't rush in and say, "Well, I own 500 acres in Texas and have 50 oil wells on it." Instead, say "Whereabouts in Indiana? What do you have there?"

If he says he has a fishing boat, don't say "Let me tell you about my private plane." Instead, ask "How long is it? Is it inboard or outboard. How long have you had it?"

"Why did you do that?"

"How did you manage that?"

"What did you say then?"

These, and similar questions, will get you a reputation as one of the most interesting talkers that your companion has ever met.

### A deadly sin in human relations and how to avoid it

Remember, human beings are innately selfish beings. They are first, last and always interested in themselves, in *their* job, *their* family, *their* home town, *their* ideas. Even a question like, "Where are *you* from?" shows that you are interested in the other person, and consequently gets him interested in you.

Don't be like the young playwright who, after talking about himself and his plays for two hours, said to his girlfriend, "But that's enough of talking about me. Let's talk about you. What do *you* think of my plays?"

Remember, you are a human being too. And it is natural for you to be tempted to start right in talking about yourself. You want to shine, you want to impress the other fellow. But the truth of the matter is that you will rate much higher in the other person's estimation if you turn the conversation to him than if you turn it to yourself. He will have a much higher opinion of you—and will consider you a much more intelligent person.

One good rule to follow is just to ask yourself mentally this question: "What do I really want in this situation?" Do you want to shine and swell your own ego—or do you want the other person's business, his name on a dotted line, his permission to do something, his good will? If all you want is to inflate your own ego, go ahead and talk exclusively about yourself but don't expect to get anything else out of the conversation.

### When to talk about yourself

Public speakers talk about themselves. They tell about their experiences, their travels, their exploits, their ideas. But remember one thing: these men are *invited* to talk about themselves. They are *asked* to talk about themselves, and the audience knows what it is in for. They do not have a captive audience, but a voluntary one. The folks who attend know in advance that they are going to hear Joe Hairychest speak on "My Adventures in the Wilds of Africa."

Unless you have hired a hall, and advertised in advance, your listeners have no way of knowing that when they talk to you they are going to be held captive and forced to listen to your exploits.

The time to talk about yourself is when you are *invited* and *asked* to tell about yourself. You can count on it that if the other person is interested, he will ask you. When he does offer you an invitation to talk about yourself, don't clam up and brush him off. Tell him a little about yourself. He'll be flattered that you are on friendly enough terms with him to let him know a little about yourself. But don't overdo it. Answer his questions—then turn the spotlight back on him.

*Use the "me-too" technique.* Another time when it is psychologically right to bring yourself into the conversation is when you can tell the other person something about yourself that will tie in to something he has said, or form a bond between you. If he says, "I was raised on a farm" and you say, "So was I," and tell a little about your farm experiences, it makes him feel more important.

If he mentions that he eats ice cream for breakfast, and it happens that you do too—by all means tell him. If he says he he was born in the little town of Swampwater, and it happens that you used to spend all your summer vacations there—tell him about it.

## The magic of agreement

The reason that bringing yourself into the conversation in a way that forms a common bond between you is flattering to the other person is this: By so doing, you are in effect saying, "I agree with you." "I am that way, too." "I like that, too." "I believe that way myself." "I am somewhat like you." Anything about you or your past experience that shows you are like the other person will help him to like you automatically.

We like people who agree with us. And we dislike people who disagree with us. Every person who agrees with us confirms our own worth and our own self-esteem. Every person who disagrees with us is a potential threat to our self-esteem. In short, when you agree with the other person, you help him to like himself better.

Even if there are points on which you know you must disagree with the other person—always seek out some points on which you can agree. When you have established some ground, however small, on which you can agree, you will find it much easier to get together on those issues on which you disagree.

## Use "Happy Talk"

Another secret of being a good conversationalist, and making people want to talk to you, is to take a tip from the song from "South Pacific" and use "Happy Talk" as much as possible.

Nobody likes a Gloomy Gus.
Nobody likes to sit and listen to a prophet of doom.
People don't like to hear bad news.

The person who falls into the habit of always talking pessimistically, of pointing out that the world is going to the dogs, or of relating all his personal troubles, isn't going to win any popularity contests.

If you have personal troubles that you need to talk over with someone, go to your pastor, your psychologist, or to some trusted and sympathetic friend. But don't air your troubles in public. Don't go on endlessly about your operation, and describe every twinge you had from the time you entered the hospital until you went back to work. Telling about how much you suffered won't make you a hero. It will only make you a bore.

### Sit right down and write yourself a letter

If you have something on your chest, and you feel as if you must tell someone all about your troubles or how unjustly you have been treated, try this:

Write yourself a letter. Put down exactly how you feel. Don't hold back anything. Go into great detail about how other people have wronged you and how unfair it is. Really make a big deal out of it.

Then, when you're all through, don't mail the letter to anyone. Burn it. It has served its purpose in giving you an outlet, and you'll find that you experience a great feeling of relief. More important for your human relations, it will drain off your emotions, and you'll no longer feel compelled to tell someone about them. Sometimes, it's necessary to write the whole thing down twice, or maybe three times. But after that, you'll find that you don't even want to think about it anymore, much less tell everyone you meet.

### What your best friend won't tell you

If you want to be popular through your conversation, try to overcome the temptation to kid, to tease, or to be sarcastic.

Most of us kid other people because we think they will like it. Husbands tease their wives in public out of the mistaken notion that it is a cute way to show affection. We make sarcastic remarks, hoping that the other fellow will recognize our cleverness, see the humor in the sarcasm, and not take personal offense.

However, teasing and kidding are both aimed at the self-esteem of the other person. And anything that threatens self-esteem is dangerous business, even when it's done in fun. Sarcasm always has a cruel element about it, and is always calculated to make the other person feel small.

Research polls have shown that people do not like to be kidded, even by their close friends. However, we do not like our friends to know we dislike kidding, for fear they will think us a poor sport. So even your best friend won't tell you that he doesn't like it.

Only in very rare instances, and between very close friends, is kidding ever taken in good grace, and then only if it is on some minor matter, and not pursued too long. If the other person has known you long enough, likes you well enough, and you do not overdo it, you may get by with kidding. But the odds are so great against it that it is much safer not to try.

### A SHORT REFRESHER ON CHAPTER 8

1. Both success and happiness depend in large measure on our ability to express ourselves. Therefore, start today to study ways to improve your talk. Keep at it day after day.

2. Practice starting conversations with strangers by using the warm-up technique of asking simple questions, or making obvious observations.

3. To be a good conversationalist, stop trying to be perfect, and don't be afraid to be trite. Nuggets and gems in conversation come only after you have dug a lot of low-grade ore.

4. Ask questions to bring out interesting talk from others.

5. Encourage the other person to talk about himself. Talk about the other person's interests.

6. Use the "me-too" technique to identify yourself with the speaker and his interests.

7. Talk about yourself only when you are invited to do so by the other person. If he wants to know about you, he'll ask.

8. Use "Happy Talk." Remember, nobody likes a Gloomy Gus or a prophet of doom. Keep your troubles to yourself.

9. Eliminate kidding, teasing, and sarcasm from your conversation.

## Chapter 9

# HOW TO USE THE TECHNIQUE THAT A
# SUPREME COURT JUSTICE CALLED
# "WHITE MAGIC"

---

WHEN A WOULD-BE POLITICIAN ASKED JUSTICE
Oliver Wendell Holmes for advice on how to get elected to
office, Justice Holmes wrote him:

> To be able to listen to others in a sympathetic and under-
> standing manner is perhaps the most effective mechanism in
> the world for getting along with people and tying up their
> friendship for good. Too few people practice the "white
> magic" of being good listeners.

In a way, each of us is "running for office" every day of our
lives. The people we meet and talk with are constantly sizing
us up, analyzing us, appraising us. In their own minds they
"vote" either for us or against us. They give us a vote of confidence or a vote of distrust. They decide in favor of doing
business with us, or not, as the case may be. More times than
you realize, the one deciding factor is—"How well did you
listen?"

You meet a certain person, and after leaving him you feel
that everything did not go just as you would have liked. You
have a sneaking suspicion that he voted against you. "What did
I say that turned him against me?" you ask yourself. Or, "What
else could I have said that would have made him more friendly,
more amenable to my ideas?"

Surprisingly enough, the answer may very well be "Nothing."
You flopped, not because of anything you said, or failed to say,
but because you failed to *listen* properly.

### Listening makes you "clever"

Most of us want the other fellow to think we are clever, intelligent, "smart."

But the person who goes around always making "smart remarks," always knocking himself out to be "clever," is not voted
in by the other fellow as a "clever person." Instead he gets
elected to the classification of "smart-aleck," "blow-hard," or
"egotist."

There is one sure way, however, to convince the other fellow
that you are one of the wisest, most intelligent persons he has
ever met. Listen, and pay attention to what *he* has to say. The
fact that you attach enough importance to what he is saying—
that you listen attentively, so as not to miss a single word—proves
to him that you are a very smart person. A dope wouldn't have
sense enough to realize how valuable and important the other
person's words are, and consequently wouldn't need to pay close
attention.

Walt Whitman and a friend were once walking down the
street, when Whitman stopped and engaged a stranger in conversation. For 15 or 20 minutes, Whitman monopolized the conversation, and the other fellow hardly opened his mouth. When
they left, Whitman turned to his friend and said, "There was
an intelligent man."

"How do you know he's intelligent?" asked his friend in surprise, "He hardly said a word."

"He listened to me, didn't he?" asked Whitman. "That proves
he is an intelligent man."

Stop to think for a moment of your friends and acquaintances.
Who has the reputation for being intelligent and wise? How do
you yourself vote on this? Do you vote for the fellow who is always shooting off his mouth? Is it the fellow who is always ready
with an answer to everything, even before he knows what the
question is? Is it the fellow who interrupts to give his answer

before the other fellow gets through talking. Or is it the fellow who does a lot of listening?

A friend of mine expresses it this way: "The Lord gave us two ears and only one mouth. Evidently He intended us to do twice as much listening as talking."

*People will tell you what they want from you, if you'll listen*

One of the nation's foremost automobile designers tells me that in order to be successful in the automobile manufacturing business you have to keep your finger on the public's pulse and keep your ears open as to what the public wants. "We don't really design our cars," he says. "The public does. What we do is listen. And when the public wants something, we hasten to try to supply it."

*You can't make a hit in the dark.* Everybody wants to make a "hit" with the other person.

You make a hit in human relations pretty much like you make a hit on a baseball diamond, by responding properly to the ball that's thrown you. You must continually make appropriate responses to what the other fellow throws you.

Good human relations consists of two-way communication. It's give and take, action and response. If you don't know what the other fellow wants, how he really feels about a situation, what his own peculiar needs are, you are out of touch with him. And if you can't touch him, you can't move him. Unless you know what he wants, and how he feels, you are completely in the dark concerning his position.

You can't make a hit in the game of human relations, anymor than you could make a hit on a basball diamond, while you'r in pitch-black darkness.

*How to use your own radar to locate the other person's position.* What the other fellow wants and how he feels need not be a mystery. "If only I knew what his position is, I'd know more what to do," we often think. Yet, it is not too difficult to find out what the other person's position is.

Al N. Sears, vice-president of Remington-Rand and chairman

of the board of National Sales Executives, says that every sales man has his own built-in radar for locating the position of prospect. "All you have to do is listen," says Al, "and he'll tel, you. Most people want us to know what their position is and try to tell us. The trouble is that we shut off our 'receiver' and start broadcasting."

### Too much talk gives you away

Sometimes there are situations in dealing with others where it is important that we not show our own hand prematurely, where we need to feel out the other fellow. The strategy used in many big business deals is to first find out what the other fellow wants, what he will settle for, before showing your own hand. It is well to remember that just as we can locate another person's position by listening to him talk, too much talk on our part gives our own position away.

Many successful businessmen, who have a reputation for being good "horse traders" and being able to "make the best bargain," have been thought to be "psychic," or mind readers.

Actually, their secret is nothing so mysterious.

They simply encourage the other person to talk—and to keep on talking—while they manage to keep their own mouths shut. They know by instinct and experience a truth which Sigmund Freud, the father of psychoanalysis, first stated scientifically. If you can get the other fellow to talk *enough*, he simply cannot disguise his real feelings or his real motives. He may try as hard as he wishes, but invariably he will "give himself away." Freu wrote a lengthy paper on unconscious slips of the tongue, show ing how the unconscious always manages to make the real feel ings and thoughts known, if you listen closely enough and re main alert to all the implications of what the other fellow says

By the same token, if you don't want the other person to know what's really on your mind—if you don't want to "show your cards" — keep your mouth shut and listen. For, no matter how you may try to disguise it, the other person will "find you out" if you just keep talking long enough.

*Listening helps overcome self-consciousness*

Another bit of "white magic" that listening can perform is to help you overcome self-consciousness and self-centeredness. Although psychology today has the different slant of "self-interest" and "self-esteem," the old attitudes of self-centeredness and self-consciousness are as much in disfavor as they ever were. Both are distinct handicaps. Listening carefully to everything the other person says—paying strict attention to his tone of voice and the inflection of his words—gets your own focus of attention off yourself.

And if all your attention is on the other fellow—what he is saying, what he wants, what his needs are—you can't be self-conscious, shut off from the other fellow. When you're shut off from him, you can't deal with him effectively. When your focus is all on yourself, you cannot deal with the world around you. You are like a man driving down the highway, who looks only *at* the windshield of his car instead of *through* the windshield to the road ahead of him. It takes no swami to predict that he is headed for a smash-up. Many head-on collisions between two people are due to the fact that one or the other had his attention on his own self rather than on the other fellow.

A strong healthy self is necessary in dealing with other people, just as a strong healthy pair of legs and feet are required of a dancer. Any good dancing teacher, however, will tell you to "get your attention off your feet" while dancing. Let a dancer become foot-conscious and think too much about his feet, let him begin to wonder whether his feet are really going to do what he wants them to do, and he is apt to stumble, or at least appear awkward and mechanical. Dancing teachers do not tell you to "cut off your feet" or "amputate your legs" just because they have discovered that paying too much attention to the feet and legs can be a handicap. In fact, they encourage their students to strengthen their legs by certain exercises. When a dancer knows that his legs are strong, and that he can depend upon them, he is more likely to be able to forget them while dancing than if he secretly fears his legs are too weak to see him through.

In much the same way, modern psychologists do not tell us anymore to deprecate the self, or overcome the self, or even to do away with all selfish instincts. What they do tell us is to get our attention off ourselves—to stop being self-centered and selfish in a petty, stupid way.

Most of the advice in the past on how to get over self-consciousness has been wrong. We have been led to believe that it is bad to care anything about the self and that we should be ashamed to admit that we have any self-regard. Since all of us do have a yearning for self-regard, this kind of advice only makes us more concerned with self than ever—and keeps our attention glued on our self and our own petty selfish desires. *The way to get over self-consciousness* is not to tell yourself that it's bad to want to think highly of yourself—but that it just doesn't work to keep all your attention *on* yourself.

A good dancer must "listen to the music." The secret of dancing, once you learn the basic steps, is not consciously to say to yourself, "Now I must be sure that my right foot goes right over here—and then I want my left foot to take one short step." If you do this, you can't listen to the music, and if you don't listen to the music, you can't keep in time or in step. A good dancer keeps his attention focused on the music the orchestra is playing and lets his feet do the right thing.

*Listen to the other fellow's music.* In dealing with other people, we need to use a similar technique. You must "listen to the music" the other fellow is playing, if you want to respond to it in a way that will create harmony instead of discords. Stop listening to his music, and begin to think to yourself, "Now what can I say that will top that?" or "How can I get in my two-cents worth to impress this fellow?"—and you get "out of step" with the other fellow.

If you'll just listen to the music and let yourself respond, you may discover something very surprising—that your own brain will work better by itself if you leave it alone, just as your feet will.

You may find that you are being more spontaneous and natural, and the really clever and appropriate things that just seem to pop out of your mouth may surprise you.

*Don't try too hard.* William James said that the reason most conversation is dull is that each party is trying too hard. When each party makes conscious effort to "think of something important" to say, he is afraid that what he has to say will not merit the approval of the other fellow. If they would but relax, said James, open their mouths and let it come out, their chances of saying something really appropriate would be increased tremendously.

According to an article in the *Saturday Evening Post,* this is the secret of Ben Thornton, famous banker and Mayor of Dallas, Texas. Thornton, says the article, has the knack of always saying the *right thing* at the *right time.* Yet, he seldom worries about what he is going to say, even goes into important meetings seemingly unprepared.

Thornton doesn't make detailed word-for-word speeches. He just prepares himself as fully as possible by gathering all the information and facts he can about the subject to be discussed. Dr. Pierce P. Brooks, who is a friend of Thornton, tells me, "He has a world of information on tap. He listens carefully to what others have to say. He feels out the other fellow. He is not satisfied to know in a general way what the other fellow wants —or what is on his mind. He wants to know exactly. After he has listened to the other fellow, he is apt to ask him to repeat some of his ideas a second time. Then, he just opens his mouth, and the right thing to fit the occasion just seems to come out automatically."

### How listening can make you rich

It has been said that listening made Ben Thornton rich People in every walk of life regard him as an understanding man. He understands people because he listens to them.

You can never really understand another human being unless you are willing to listen, carefully, sympathetically, and patiently.

This kind of listening can make you rich, too . . . rich in dollars, rich in friends, rich in the satisfaction of accomplishment and happiness.

One of the highest compliments you can pay another person

is simply to listen to him. By your patient listening you say to him, "You are *worth* listening to." You increase his self-esteem, for every human being likes to think he "has something to say" that is worth saying.

On the other hand, one of the most deflating things you can do to the other fellow's ego is to brush him off before hearing what he has to say. Remember, people like to be "paid attention to."

Ever hear a wife say of her husband, "He never hears a word I say. I could say to him 'the hot water tank just blew up' and all he'd say would be 'Is that right?' and go right on reading his paper." Maybe you haven't heard this, but marital counselors hear it every day.

Ever hear an employee say, "I would like my boss fine, except he just won't listen. I go to him to tell him about a problem and ask his advice and before I get half-way through he interrupts and gives me a pat answer before he even knows what I'm talking about. He's not a bad guy, if he would just listen."

Maybe you haven't heard those words, but grievance committees in industry hear them over and over.

Ever hear a young person say, "My parents don't really understand me at all. I try to tell them how I really feel about things, what my problems are, but they just won't listen. They either treat me like a child and brush off my problems as having no importance—or else they are so anxious to tell me how I ought to feel about things, they never know how I really feel." Juvenile court judges hear that same theme, with variations, every day.

A lot of trouble, misery, and failure happens in our world just because someone wouldn't listen.

Keep this bit of advice pasted up on the wall of your mind, where you can see it at all times:

> *You've Got to Know What People Want, What*
> *They Need, and What They Are*

—if you are going to deal with them effectively. This applies to enemies as well as to friends. It applies to children, grown-ups, big shots, and small-fry. And the way to know what people want, need and are is simply LISTEN TO THEM.

## Seven Ways to Practice Listening

This art of listening is so important, don't pass it over without putting it into practice. Perhaps you read something that sounds good, are convinced it's true, then resolve to put it into practice. But if you don't check yourself, you forget all about it in a day or two. One way to overcome this is to list some definite things to do and start doing them.

So "nail-down" the knowledge you gained in this chapter, and don't let it get away. Starting right now, practice the following:

1. **Look at the person who is talking.**

    Anybody worth listening to is worth looking at. It'll also help you concentrate on what he's saying.

2. **Appear deeply interested in what he is saying.**

    If you agree, nod your head. If he tells a story, smile. Respond to his cue. Work with him.

3. **Lean toward the person who is talking.**

    Ever notice you have a tendency to lean toward an interesting talker, and lean away from a dull one?

4. **Ask questions.**

    This lets the person who is talking know that you are are still listening.

5. **Don't interrupt; instead, ask him to tell more.**

    Most people are highly complimented if you don't interrupt them until they're through. But they're doubly complimented if you draw them out. "Would you mind going into that last point a little more fully?" —or "I'd like to know a little more about what you were saying concerning such and such."

6. **Stick to the speaker's subject.**

    Don't change subjects on a person until he is finished, no matter how anxious you are to get started on a new one.

7. **Use the speaker's words to get your own point across.**

    When the other fellow has finished talking—repeat

back to him some of the things he has said. This not only proves you've been listening, but is a good way to introduce your own ideas without opposition.

Preface some of your own remarks with, "As you pointed out—." or "It's just like you said—."

Chapter 10

# HOW TO GET OTHERS TO SEE THINGS
# YOUR WAY . . . QUICKLY!

---

Every day, some situation arises wherein we need to persuade another person to accept our own viewpoint. Some point of disagreement comes up with wife, husband, child, boss, neighbor, customer, employee, friend, or enemy.

"If only I could get him to see things my way," we say.

Take these instances:

1. Suppose you are a clerk in a retail store and a customer comes in and demands that he be given a new refrigerator for the one he purchased, two months after the guarantee period has expired. You try to explain that the company will repair the old refrigerator, but cannot give a brand new one. The customer cannot see this. How do you settle this difference of opinion?

2. You are in a conference and your boss comes up with an idea for sales promotion that seems good on the surface. However, you see several serious flaws in the idea, and realize that it may well cost the company too much money and lose more customers than it gains. How do you go about convincing your boss that his idea won't work?

3. Your wife wants to send your son to a private school. There are many reasons that lead you to believe he will be better off in public school. How do you go about getting these ideas across?

4. You feel that you deserve a raise and that the company

104

can well afford to pay you more. You mention the idea, and your boss says "We can't afford it now; see me later." What do you say?

## Why the "Natural Way" is wrong

The natural thing to do when we run up against a contrary idea or opinion is to argue. It may be only a question of which baseball team is the best — or it may be a question debated by statesmen in the United Nations. Unfortunately, the natural thing is still to attempt to argue down our opponent.

Someone has said that golf is difficult because the golf swing is unnatural. It goes against every natural impuse of how to swing a club. We must learn a scientific, but unnatural swing.

The same thing might be said for the art of persuasion. It is natural to regard someone who opposes our ideas as an opponent to be overcome in one way or another. Yet, what we really want to do is convince the other fellow, induce him to change his mind rather than to conquer him or beat him down.

When someone opposes our ideas, it is natural for us to take it as a threat and a slap to our own ego. And so it is natural to hit back at his own ego, to become emotional and hostile, to shout, threaten, shame, ridicule, and try to ram our ideas down his throat by intimidation or force. We exaggerate every one of our own so-called reasons or claims, and make light of every one of our opponent's points.

But this natural way does not win. Because the only way you can ever really win an argument is to get the other fellow to change his mind.

## Science discovers a way to win arguments

The old saying, "Nobody ever won an argument" is true if you mean by argument the shouting session, or the ego battle. However, there are ways that you can induce the other fellow to see things your way.

The way to win an argument scientifically, however, is just the opposite method that most of us naturally use. Even organizations that want to get the general public to change its ideas usually make the same mistakes that you and I make when we are arguing about baseball or politics.

"Why," asks *Science Digest* (March, 1954) "is the American public so reluctant to support an adequate civil defense program in view of the repeated demonstrations of the dangers of unpreparedness? And why do so many cancer patients avoid treatment until it is too late, despite all the dramatic warnings issued about the need for early care? One important factor may be that appeals which arouse intense fears, or which constitute threats, are not effective in persuading people to change their opinions or behavior. This was revealed in a series of 25 experiments conducted by three Yale psychologists."

### *Low pressure is the secret*

These three Yale psychologists, Carl I. Hovland, Irving L. Janis, and Harold H. Kelly, found that the best way to get ideas accepted is to use a low-pressure technique, one of calmly presenting facts, and leaving out threats or attempts at using force.

In one experiment, an illustrated 15-minute lecture on dental hygiene was given to three different groups of students. The first group got a "strong" appeal, pointing up the dangers of dental neglect: tooth decay, diseased gums, cancer, and the like.

The second group received a "moderate" appeal, in which the dangers were presented, but in a milder and more factual way.

The third group received a lecture presenting straight information that hardly touched at all on the dangers of neglect.

A week after the talks were given, the students were checked to see which ones had modified their behavior most and were following the practices recommended in the talks. Surprisingly enough, the students who heard the "soft" appeal, with no scare tactics, were more closely following the practices outlined in the lectures than those who had heard the "scare appeal."

Other tests with college students have shown similar results in political arguments. It was found that students were more likely to change their political opinions if the "other side" presented unemotional facts than if they made wild harangues.

*The amazing fact that a scientific analysis of 10,000 actual arguments produced*

Perhaps the most exhaustive research work that has ever been done on arguments was performed by Professors Alvin C. Busse and Richard C. Borden, formerly with New York University's Speech Department.

These professors listened to 10,000 actual arguments over a seven-year period. They listened to hassles between taxi-drivers, between husbands and wives. Macy's, Westinghouse, and other business firms cooperated and allowed them to eavesdrop on salesmen and counter clerks. They listened to debates in the U.N. They made notes of who won the argument, and why.

They came to the interesting conclusion that professional debaters — politicians, U.N. delegates — were less successful than door-to-door salesmen in getting their ideas accepted.

The one big reason turned out to be that the professional debaters seemed to be intent upon beating down the opposition, or "showing up" the opposing argument, whereas the salesman was trying to induce the prospect to want to change his own mind.

They found that the one big mistake most of us make in trying to win an argument is in *attacking the ego of the other person.*

*How to persuade by working with human nature*

It all boils down to the theme of this book: you must learn to work with human nature, rather than against it, if you want to have power with people.

Tell a man that his ideas are stupid, and he will defend them all the more. Ridicule his position, and he has to defend it to save face. Use threats, or scare tactics, and he simply closes his mind against your ideas, regardless of how good they may be.

One of the strongest urges in human nature is self-survival, and this means survival of the ego as well as the body. For our own protection, we have to be careful of the ideas that we accept and act upon. We learn to immunize ourselves against any idea that is seen as an enemy. Friends don't usually come

at us hammer-and-tongs, and so to be safe we just close our ears
to ideas that come to us dressed up like enemies.

### How to reach the other person's subsconscious mind

When we attempt to sell ideas, we are really trying to reach
the other person's subconscious, because no idea is really accepted and acted upon *until the subconscious mind accepts it.*
"A man convinced against his will is of the same opinion still"
describes the man or woman who has accepted an idea with the
conscious mind—but not with the subconscious. Such a person
may give lip service to the idea and appear to agree with you,
but he is still unconvinced and *will not act* on the idea.

*There is just one way to get an idea accepted* by the subconscious mind, psychologists know, and that is *by suggestion.*
Numerous experiments have shown that the harder you try to
force an idea into the subconscious—the more resistance that
idea meets. It is the old instinct of self-preservation at work
again. The technique used by psychologists is to "slip" the idea
into the subconscious mind—more or less unnoticed.

Ever notice that when someone tells you, "You can't do that,"
you have an irresistible impulse to do it anyway? Ever notice
that when someone tells you "You have got to do so and so,"
you almost automatically react by saying to yourself, "I'll be
darned if I do!"

### Six Tested Rules for Winning Arguments

You will be successful in winning arguments to the degree
that you are successful in slipping your ideas past the ego of
the other person. His ego is like a guard that stands at the en-
trance of his subconscious mind. If you wake up his ego, or
arouse it too much, his ego simply will not let your ideas past.
This is the all-important point. Keep it in mind as you study
the following points:

### 1. Let him state his case

Don't interrupt. Let him state his case. Remember the magic
of listening. It not only wounds the other person's ego to be

interrupted and brushed off; we run into what the psychologists call *mental set*. The person with something on his chest has his mental set all geared for talking. And until he has said his piece, his mental set is not tuned for listening to your ideas. If you want your own ideas to be heard, learn to listen first to the other fellow.

John Graham, director of personnel of F. & R. Lazarus & Company, Columbus, Ohio, is one of the most skillful persuaders I have ever met. When his ideas meet opposition, or when someone has a complaint to make, he always hears the other fellow out. He then goes one step further by asking the other person to repeat some of his points, and by asking whether there is anything else he would like to say. This shows the other person that he is interested in his point of view.

Asking the other person to repeat his key points is also valuable when the other person comes to you hot under the collar. Merely letting him get it off his chest goes a long way to reduce his feeling of hostility. If you can get him to "play back" his complaint two or three times, it drains off virtually all his emotion or steam.

## 2. *Pause before you answer*

This rule works equally well in conversation where there is no apparent difference of opinion. When someone asks you a question, look at him and pause slightly before answering. This will let the other person know that you consider what he has said of sufficient importance to "think about it," or "consider it."

A slight pause is all that is needed. Pause too long, and you give the impression that you are hemming and hawing, or trying to evade giving a definite answer. If you must disagree with a person, however, the slight pause is important. Come out with a fast "no," and the other fellow feels that you are not interested enough to take time with his problems.

## 3. *Don't insist on winning 100 per cent*

Most of us, when we get into an argument, attempt to prove that we are totally and completely right, and the other fellow

is wrong on all points. Skillful persuaders, however, always con-
cede *something* and find some point of agreement.

If the other person has a point in his favor, acknowledge it.
And if you give in on minor and unimportant points, the other
fellow will be much more likely to give in when you come to
the big question.

David Babcock, vice-president and director of personnel of
The Dayton Company, Minneapolis, one of the largest stores
in America, uses this rule to perfection. If he cannot grant a
request of an employee, he always explains "why." If he must
shift an employee from one department to another he doesn't
just say, "Miss Smith, I am transferring you to another department as of tomorrow morning." He tells Miss Smith why she
is being transferred.

Dr. Pierce P. Brooks, president of National Banker's Life
Insurance Company, Dallas, Texas, and author of *How Power
Selling Brought Me Success in Six Hours,* recommends what he
calls the "yes—but" technique.

"Yes, I can see you have a good point there, but have you
considered this. . . ."

"Yes, I can understand why it might appear that way, but. . . ."

"Yes, you are certainly right about that all right, but on the
other hand. . . ."

### 4. State your case moderately and accurately

The tendency that we have to watch in trying to get our
ideas accepted, when they are opposed, is to exaggerate and
make too forceful an appeal. Remember that scientifically
proved tests show that calmly stated facts are more effective in
getting people to change their minds than are threats and force.

One reason we still use the old forceful methods is that they
sometimes *seem* to work. You beat the other fellow down. You
show him up. You get him to the point where "he can't say a
thing." Your audience applauds, and you think you have won
the argument. But the other fellow still hasn't accepted your
viewpoint, and he will not act upon your ideas.

Benjamin Franklin is generally conceded to have been one

of the best idea salesmen of all time. In dealing with foreign nations, he always came out on top, and got what he wanted. He is credited with having put across, against much opposition, the Constitution of the United States.

"The way to convince another," said Franklin, "is to state your case moderately and accurately. Then say that of course you may be mistaken about it; which causes your listener to receive what you have to say, and, like as not, turn about and convince you of it, since you are in doubt. But if you go at him in a tone of positiveness and arrogance you only make an opponent of him."

The same psychology works—whether you are trying to get an assembly to adopt your views on something as important as signing the Constitution of the United States, or whether you would like your husband or wife to accept your views on how to decorate the house.

### 5. Speak through third persons

The lawyer who wants to win cases rounds up witnesses who will testify to the points he wants to put over to the jury. He realizes that the argument is more convincing if disinterested third persons say that such-and-such happened, rather than if *he* says it.

The star salesman uses testimonials of satisfied users. The candidate for public office gets well-known organizations and individuals to endorse him. If *he* says, "I'm the most honest, most intelligent, and best qualified candidate in this race," voters may have their doubts. But if the League of Upright Citizens says the same thing, it is likely to carry a lot of weight.

Applicants for positions carry "recommendations" from third parties that are a lot more convincing to the prospective employer than anything the applicant could say in his own behalf.

Speaking through third persons is especially valuable when you have a difference of opinion and want the other fellow to see things your way. For one thing, people are naturally skeptical of you when you are saying things to your own advantage. Equally important is the fact that what third persons say is much less likely to arouse the ego of the other person than what you say. Records, statistics, history, a quotation from some well-known person, can all be cited as third persons.

Let's say your wife wants the new house drapes to be all the same color, whereas you would like them to be different. If you say, "I think it is old-fashioned and behind the times to have drapes all the same color," you are going to start an argument. "Oh. So now I'm old-fashioned and behind the times," she'll say.

But if you say, "I was listening to Peter Lind Hayes on the radio the other day and he was telling about how he and Mary had furnished their place with different colored drapes. He said it was getting to be old-fashioned to have all the drapes the same color," you do not arouse any antagonism, and you cite an endorsement at the same time.

Not long ago I purchased an automobile liability insurance policy. When I saw that the salesman had quoted me prices on a $100,000 policy, I was a little irritated. I thought he was trying to slip one over on me.

"I didn't say anything about $100,000," I protested. "I just want the customary $25,000 policy."

"But the $100,000 policy *is* the customary policy, now," he said. "About 90 per cent of our new policy-holders get the $100,000 policy. Civil court juries are awarding much higher judgments than they used to. And $50,000 and $100,000 judgments are now getting to be ordinary."

He saved an argument and changed my mind by letting third persons speak for him. I couldn't very well argue with 90 per cent of his new policy-holders and civil court juries.

When you ask the boss for a raise it will carry more weight if you say, "I believe my record here will show that I have earned a raise," rather than, "I believe I deserve a raise."

## 6. Let the other person save face

Many times the other fellow would gladly change his mind and agree with you, except for one thing. He has already made a definite commitment—come out with a strong stand, and he cannot change his position in good grace. To agree with you would be to admit he was wrong. And if he has already made definite strong statements opposing your view, he would almost have to admit that he had lied.

Skillful persuaders know how to leave the door open so that the other fellow can escape from his previous position without losing face. They leave a loophole that the other fellow can go through. Otherwise, he may find himself a prisoner of his own logic. He cannot escape from his own previous stand. If you would persuade another, you must not only convince him. You must also know how to rescue him from his own argument.

Here are two ways:

*Method No. 1.* Assume that the other person did not have all the facts to begin with. "Of course, I can well understand how you might have thought so-and-so, since you did not know about such-and-such at the time."

If the other fellow was wrong, find some excuse for his being wrong.

"Anybody would have thought the same thing under the circumstances."

"I felt the same way about it at first, but then I ran across this information which changes the whole picture."

*Method No. 2.* Suggest some way that he can pass the buck to some other person. A customer of a department store returns a dress. She took it home and her husband did not like it. "It has never been worn," she says.

The sales clerk examines the dress and sees that it shows definite signs of having been dry-cleaned. Now, the sales clerk can show the customer the evidence and prove she is wrong, but she will never admit it, because she has already gone on record as saying, "It has never been worn." So the smart sales-clerk gives Mrs. Customer a loophole through which she can escape.

The sales clerk says, "Mrs. Customer, I wonder if some member of your family could have sent this dress to the cleaners by mistake. I know the same thing happened to me not long ago. I was out when the cleaning man came and my husband sent a brand new dress out and had it cleaned, along with some other dresses I had in the same closet. I wonder if this could have happened to you — because this dress does show definite signs of having been cleaned."

Mrs. Customer sees the evidence — she knows she is wrong — and she has a ready-made excuse for being wrong. There is an open door through which she can escape.

### CHAPTER 10 IN A NUTSHELL

When you have a difference of opinion with someone, your object should not be to "win an argument," but to get the other person to change his own mind and see things your way. Thus, you must avoid bringing his ego into play. You must slip your "logical reasons" past his ego, then clinch it by leaving him a loophole through which he can escape from his previous position.

The following six rules will help you accomplish this:

1. Let him state his case.
2. Pause momentarily before you answer.
3. Don't insist on winning 100 per cent.
4. State your case moderately and accurately.
5. Speak through third persons.
6. Let the other fellow save face.

# Part Five

# HOW TO MANAGE PEOPLE SUCCESSFULLY

---

# Chapter 11

# HOW TO GET 100 PER CENT COOPERATION AND INCREASE YOUR BRAIN POWER

---

**W**ILL YOU TRY A SIMPLE TWO-STEP EXPERIMENT the next time you want someone to help you do something? It doesn't matter whether the job is mowing your lawn, tying up a package, or making your business successful.

*Step 1.* First, simply ask someone to, "Help me *do* this." Tell them what they are expected to do. Offer to pay them to help, if you want, but make it plain they are to be paid only to carry out your own ideas. Make a note of the cooperation you get, and the success of your joint efforts.

*Step 2.* Next, approach somebody else and ask for help. Only this time don't just ask the other fellow to help you "do" the job, but also ask him to help you "think" about the job. Ask for his ideas as well as his brawn.

Say, "I've got a problem here and I need your help. Here is what I want to accomplish. What do you think about it? Do you have any ideas I could use? What is your opinion of the way I am going about this?"

Again, judge the results.

Invariably, you will find that although you may get *some* cooperation and help by using the first method, you get 100 per cent *cooperation* and much more *actual physical work* from the other person, by using the second method.

*How to get the other fellow to go all out*

Why is it that if you are out spading your lawn and you say

to your neighbor, "Joe, how about helping me spade this lawn?" he will tell you to go jump in the lake?

But if you say, "Joe, I've got a problem here. I wish I knew what I'm doing wrong. I can't seem to get the knack of preparing this ground properly so grass will grow on it. Do you have any ideas of anything that would help." Joe is very likely to come over, take the spade out of your hands, and say, "Here, let me show you how to spade a lawn."

The reason is simple. By using the second approach you are working in harmony with a basic law of human nature. Industrial psychologists have discovered that it is not so much a question that Joe *won't* help you, he *can't* go all out in helping you, unless he gets his brain and his brawn both working on the job.

**It is psychologically impossible for a human being to give us 100 per cent of his brawn, unless he is also allowed to give us his *ideas*.**

It is as if the brain and the body have decided to work together as a team. And, as they said in vaudeville, neither will "break up the act, and do a single."

This has been proved beyond doubt by records kept on industrial workers. Workers who have no voice whatsoever in management, who cannot make suggestions, who are not allowed to contribute their ideas, simply do not do as much work as workers who are encouraged to make suggestions.

### Make them feel it's their problem, too

All of us are interested in our own problems more than the other fellow's problems. When you simply ask Joe to help you spade your lawn, his feeling is, "That's your problem." But when you ask Joe's advice and suggestions, you have challenged him — you have in effect given *him* a problem to solve, and he becomes interested. This principle works in getting your lawn spaded. It works in running your business.

For example, one of the toughest problems management has in business is getting department heads to cut costs. It's a big problem in any business. Some businesses try preachments; some try appealing to duty. But keeping down expenses is commonly regarded as one of the biggest problems, and one that business men get the least amount of cooperation on.

When 35-year-old Robert C. Hood, head of Ansul Chemical Company, Marinette, Wisconsin, was faced with this problem, he didn't preach or scold. He didn't just tell workers they had to "cut costs." His management philosophy is: "People support what they help create." So when he wanted to cut costs, he formed a committee of all the top operations people in his company. He didn't tell them they had to cut down on any specific item here or there. Instead, he told them it was *their* problem to work out ideas of their own.

The committee members got their heads together and began to come up with ideas for saving money on travel, use of telephone and telegraph, supplies, and even postage. A short time ago Mr. Hood reported to the American Management Association, the results of this program, which "enabled us to reduce costs to such an extent that profits after taxes increased by 40 per cent even in a period when sales were showing a 9 per cent increase."

Hood uses this same principle to solve many other business problems. He calls it *participative management.*

### How to use participative management in the home

How many wives have you heard complain that their husbands never tell them anything about their business or their plans? Never give them a chance to make suggestions. Yet, you hear husbands say that their wives will not cooperate in saving money, and so on. Many parents believe that their children won't cooperate in something the parent wants done, yet they never *ask* the child to participate, but only *tell* him to "do so and so." They never ask the child to contribute any ideas, only his physical actions.

Marital counselors have adopted a technique for getting cooperation in the home that is very similar to participative management in industry. It is called "Family Planning Sessions."

The wife, husband, and children get together for a family conference once a week, or once a month. The important thing is that the entire family holds regular meetings during which problems are discussed, common goals are set out, and each member of the family is asked to contribute ideas.

Dr. Ruth Barbee said to me recently, "It is amazing what can be accomplished when the entire family participates in managing the family. 'Impossible situations' become ironed out satisfactorily, the family gets along better together, and everyone is happier, when each member is not just told to 'do this or that' but is asked to make the problem his own problem and figure out some idea *how* we can do this or that. No other one method that I know of has ever had the success that Family Planning Sessions has achieved."

She goes on to point out that the family, just as a business concern, must have one chief executive whose job it is to weigh the many suggestions that come in and make final decisions.

"However," she says, "it is surprising how willingly a child will accept the final authority of the father, even if the decision goes against him, *provided* he has had a chance to voice his opinions, and make his suggestions, before the final decision is reached."

Business executives have found the same to be true.

### Why not multiply your own brain power 10 or 100 times?

It used to be thought that the job of management was to furnish all the ideas and all the brains. Management was the brains of the outfit, and employees were merely hands. However, the best management men today realize that the best brains are not concentrated exclusively in the front office. Men and women in the plant have ideas, or could have if they were given incentive to have them. The best executives today are not afraid to ask a worker for an idea or a suggestion, out of fear that someone will get the idea that he is not smart enough to run the business. He *knows* that he is not smart enough to come up with all the good ideas that 100 of his workers could think up — if encouraged to do so. So he is constantly asking his workers,

"What is your opinion?" or "How could we do this better?" and pays them extra for their ideas.

The ideal business executive today is not a man who is a genius, not a man who is so smart that he has all the ideas that are possible. He is a man smart enough to avail himself of the countless ideas of the men working under him, and with the administrative ability to make final decisions and see them put into action. He *is* a genius all right, but in *human relations* rather than in creative ideas. He knows how to multiply his own ideas by the ideas of others. He knows how to manage people, get them to abide by his decisions, and put his decisions into operation wholeheartedly.

### How 'the power of people' multiplied McCormick's sales 1500 per cent

In its September, 1951 issue, *Investor's Reader* ran an article called "Management: The Power of People." It illustrates the difference between the old-style management methods and the new. It tells about a company that used both, and the amazing results that followed when the new methods were used.

In 1931, Christmas at Baltimore's McCormick & Company was the sad affair it had been for years. Notices were given of a layoff 'until about February 1' along with the ironic wish 'Merry Christmas and a Happy New Year'!

In 1950 the employees of McCormick & Company's Baltimore plant worked pell-mell right up to the day before Christmas, then left for home with a whoop and a holler. And no wonder: in their pockets was two weeks extra cash bonus and ahead of them a full-paid winter vacation until January 2. The bonus was an addition to three weeks extra already paid that year; the vacation was in addition to the regular summer vacation and seven paid holidays.

The contrast between these two situations is the degree of success achieved in less than 20 years by one man and one idea. The man is perspicacious, 55-year-old Charles Perry McCormick, chairman and president of 'the world's largest spice and extract business.' The idea is 'multiple management,' an operating system designed to insure maximum worker participation and morale to say nothing of providing management with a seedbed of youthful and ambitious executive talent.

The story actually starts way back in 1889, when Charlie's uncle, Willoughby McCormick, started his spice business in a dingy room with two employees. 'Uncle Will' was a hard worker and a hard boss. Sales reached $3,500,000 in 1932 but employes were listless and dispirited. Labor turnover was an expensive 30 per cent a year.

Nephew Charlie ('The Old Man' had no children) started working at the plant in summers in 1912, came on full time in 1919. He worked as stock boy, runner, an executive assistant in factory and office, and for over ten years as salesman and export sales executive. He also tried to sell Uncle Will some new management ideas but was fired seven times for his trouble (he was also rehired). Came the Great Depression and big losses for McCormick. As was the tenor of the times, the Old Man slashed wages 25 per cent and had another 10 per cent ax in hand when he suddenly died on a business trip in 1932.

Since it did not seem to make much difference who headed the hard-pressed concern, the directors elected young Charlie. The practical prophet decided to use some of his ideas. He called a meeting of all employees and announced a 10 per cent raise instead of a cut and a work week shortened from 56 to 46 hours. He also told the workers they had to raise production and cut costs or the whole kit and caboodle might collapse. To help them along he told his astonished employees they would henceforth share in the profits of the company and take an active part in management.

The active part consisted of a junior board of directors and the beginnings of multiple management. The first board had 17 members (credit clerks, cost accountants, assistant department heads). Their assignment was to find ways and means to improve anything they thought needed it. In addition: 'write your own constitution and by-laws, elect your own officers and govern yourself as you wish. The company books are open to you and ask all the questions you like.'

To keep things under control, Charlie said all suggestions must be unanimous and subject to approval of the senior board (the stockholder board elected annually).

The idea clicked. Within a few years the junior board had redesigned and modernized the company's packages with a resultant sharp rise in sales; they devised new ways to test stenographers; they introduced faster and better billing machines; they suggested new product lines from pumpkin pie spice to the recently introduced fast-selling cinnamon sugar.

As a good spice man, Charlie likes to say 'the proof of the pudding is in the eating.' On that basis the junior board has quite a record: of 5,000 suggestions made, over 99 per cent have been adopted by the senior board. Says Charlie: 'I cannot estimate how much these suggestions have meant to this company in increased sales and profits but certainly the benefits far exceed the cost.' More important, the junior board has bolstered morale and given all ambitious young men a chance to be a company officer and director. The goal is attainable since no less than 13 of the present 17-man senior board were formerly junior or factory board members.

How has this "multiple management" worked out at McCormick? Under old methods of management, "Uncle Will" — the boss who ruled with an iron hand, managed to get sales up to 3½ million dollars. Which sounds like a pretty good endorsement of the old methods, until you realize that by enlisting the brains as well as the brawn of the workers, Charlie McCormick increased sales volume about 15 times to around 50 million dollars a year. "When we started," says Charlie McCormick, "we had a small sales volume, no profits, no dividends, no employee morale, no rest periods, no vacations, no profit sharing and no retirement fund."

### How to get others to support your ideas

Very often we need the "yes," "O. K.," or endorsement of another person to get some idea of our own adopted. The best way in the world to get this support is to get the other fellow to participate *in* your idea.

Instead of saying, "I wish you would approve this," or, "I wish you would decide in my favor," try saying this: "If you were me, how would you go about getting this idea across?"

I know an army colonel today, West Point, Class of 1933, who has this technique to thank for his whole career.

All his life he had dreamed of going to West Point. He was graduated from high school just as the depression of 1929 hit. Many parents who normally could have afforded to send their sons to college could no longer do so and many of these sons were competing for the free education at West Point and Annapolis.

My friend had no connections whatsoever. So he went to several of the most prominent figures in his state and asked them a simple question. "Mr. ———, if you were in my position and you wanted to go to West Point and were thoroughly qualified for it, what would you do?"

That "What would you do?" was asking for their ideas. It asked for their participation in the problem. And essentially it made his problem their problem. He got not only their recommendations, but their active help, and he got the appointment.

Had this young man gone to these men and merely asked for their endorsements the chances would have been small, for he was a nobody, a nonentity. By asking for their advice instead, he got their endorsement.

### Set up your own brain trust

One of the wealthiest men I have ever known once told me that he owed his success to the fact that he had learned something from almost everyone he had ever come in contact with. One of his first business ventures was the operation of a saw-mill.

"My employees were illiterates," he told me. "Some of them could not even sign their own names. But I knew that they had worked at this game for a long time and must have their own ideas. I made it a point to learn what they knew, and ask for their ideas."

Later on, this man applied this same principle in the operation of a bank, a department store, and several other businesses.

"If I've made money," he said, "it's not because of my own

brains, but because of my 'brain trust': the ideas I got from other people. Not only have I gotten many good ideas in this way, but it compliments the other person. It always flatters the other person to ask his advice and to seek his ideas."

Try this technique on your friends, family, associates, and co-workers. See how the other fellow brightens up when you ask for his advice. See how he warms up to you when you say, "What is your opinion about this matter?" or "How would you go about doing this?"

Try this technique as a door-opener. The next time you want to get in to see someone difficult to see, send in word that you want to consult with him and get his opinion about a certain matter!

A magazine writer who writes articles for the slicks tells me that he often uses a variation of this technique to get an interview with a big shot who has the reputation of being hard to see.

He merely calls on the phone and says, "Mr. X, you've been referred to me as an authority on the subject of ————. I'm trying to prepare an article on this matter and everyone I talk with tells me that if I want to get the real facts about this matter, I should see you and get your ideas."

### The Magic Secret of Asking for Advice

As you read this, you may be thinking of some individual who is always asking other people for advice, always telling his troubles and problems to others, and succeeding only in making a nuisance of himself. Maybe you're wondering how a technique that can make one man wealthy and prosperous can make another man a failure.

The magic secret of using this technique is this: It depends on *why* you ask.

There is a certain type of person who is always telling others his troubles, and constantly asking for advice. He doesn't solve his problems. He makes a nuisance of himself. Instead of becoming popular by using this technique, he is someone avoided by others.

Such a person is not actually seeking advice. He wants sym

pathy or pity. When he asks you "What in the world am I going to do?" he doesn't expect you to tell him. He would be insulted if you did. He expects only that you feel sorry for him and tell him he is in the worst plight of any human being you have ever heard of. He wants you to agree that he has been treated unjustly. But the last thing he wants is an answer to his problem. And if you doubt this, next time ask him, "Why don't you try so and so?" and watch his reaction.

There is also the individual who comes apparently asking for advice and opinion, but who really wants a pat on the back. A popular song-writer tells me that people he knows often say to him, "Here is a song I have written. I wish you would look it over and tell me what you think of it, or if it needs any improvement."

"I lost two or three good friends," he told me, "before I discovered that these people don't really want my *opinion,* and they wouldn't take my advice if I gave it. What they want is a pat on the back. They think they have written a pretty good song, and they want my assurance that it is as good as they would like to think it is."

So remember this: Ask the other fellow for advice, ideas, suggestions, and *really mean it.* You not only will get some good suggestions to help you solve your problem, but you compliment the other fellow as well.

Don't ask for advice when all you want is assurance that you are right. Don't ask for advice or opinions when all you want is sympathy. If you do, you not only will fail to get anywhere solving your problems — you'll make a nuisance of yourself as well.


### THE MEAT IN THE COCONUT FOR CHAPTER 11

1. If you want other people to help you, and go all out, you must ask for their ideas as well as for their brawn.
2. Make the other fellow feel that *your* problem is *his* problem.
3. Use the principle of *multiple management,* giving each member of the team a voice in how the team is to operate.

4. When you want someone to do you a favor, make him
   a member of your team. Don't just say, "How about
   putting in a good word for me." Say, "If you were in
   my shoes and wanted to get favorable attention, how
   would you go about it?"
5. Set up your own brain trust, and make use of the ideas,
   suggestions, and advice of other people.
6. Be sure when you ask for advice you actually want
   advice. Don't ask for advice if all you want is sympathy or a pat on the back.

Suggestion: Make it a point to apply these six rules for one
            week in your home, your office, your club, and
            keep a record of the results you obtain.

# Chapter 12

# HOW TO USE YOUR MIRACLE POWER IN HUMAN RELATIONS

---

Do you believe in miracles? if not, you may be surprised to learn that many medical doctors and scientists today believe in miracles, even if they cannot understand them.

Dr. John R. Brobeck, professor of physiology at the University of Pennsylvania, recently read a paper on miracles and science before the British and Canadian Medical Associations. He said in substance that the one factor today that science cannot understand about miracles is: What is the source of *energy* for miracles?

Dr. Alexis Carrel, the famous scientist, also wrote a scientific paper on miracles, and commented on the fact that ordinary "natural" healing processes appeared to be tremendously speeded up through some sudden and tremendous inrush of energy, not known to natural science. Dr. Carrel believed that this energy was a spiritual power.

*How praise releases energy*

All through the ages, many people have believed that *praise* has some sort of miracle-working power. Charles Fillmore, cofounder of Unity School of Christianity, wrote, "Words of praise, gratitude, or thanksgiving expand, set free, and in every way radiate energy.... You can praise a weak body into strength, a fearful heart into peace and trust; shattered nerves into pois and power; a failing business into prosperity and success; want and insufficiency into supply and support."

Did you ever notice in the Bible how often *praise* and *thanksgiving* are associated with miracles? Before Elisha miraculously increased the widow's oil, he *blessed it* and gave thanks. Before Jesus multiplied the loaves and fishes he *blessed them,* lifted his eyes to Heaven and gave *thanks.*

"There is an inherent law of mind that we increase whatever we praise," Charles Fillmore said. "The whole of creation responds to praise and is glad. Animal trainers pet and reward their charges with delicacies for acts of obedience; children glow with joy and gladness when they are praised. Even vegetation grows better for those who love it."

Just how praise releases energy, no one seems to know. But the fact that it does is common experience. Ever notice how, when someone pays you a sincere compliment, or thanks you for a job well done, your spirits seem to get a shot in the arm?

I used to know a grand old lady who would say, everytime someone complimented her on how fine she looked, "Thank you, I can live another year on that." She might not have been far wrong. For praise does give us new energy, and new life.

The lift that you get from praise is not an illusion. Neither is it just your imagination. In some way, unknown to science, actual physical energy is released.

Dr. Henry H. Goddard, when he was psychologist at Vineland Training School in New Jersey, used an instrument he called the "ergograph" to measure fatigue. When tired children were given a word of praise or commendation, the ergograph showed an immediate upward surge of new energy. When the children were criticized and discouraged, the ergograph showed that their physical energy took a sudden nosedive. So, even though science cannot explain the power of praise, science can measure it!

*How to apply praise to human relations*

At this point you may very well say, "Well, that is certainly interesting about how praise releases energy, and gives the other fellow a lift, in some miraculous way that science cannot understand, but what has that got to do with getting along with people?"

The answer is, "Everything."

Remember our motto — "LSMFT" (Low Self-esteem Means Friction and Trouble)?

Well, here is an almost magical way to overcome friction and trouble by literally giving the other person's self-esteem a spiritual shot in the arm.

Several years ago Charles G. Nichols, president of G. M. McKelvey Co., Youngstown, Ohio and the author were talking about the fact that cantankerous and hard-to-get-along-with people are usually suffering from a lack of self-esteem.

"Wouldn't it be a wonderful thing," I said, "if someone would discover a wonder drug for the human spirit — a sort of ego tonic that you could carry around in your pocket? Whenever you met someone who was discouraged, had a chip on his shoulder, or wanted to give you a hard time, you could just give him a dose from your bottle. He would begin to think more highly of himself — his self-esteem would perk up — and presto! he would become friendly and cooperative."

"There is such a tonic, Les," he told me. "And believe me it is every bit as amazing in its results as any wonder drug. This wonder drug is *praise* — giving the other fellow credit — letting him know his efforts are appreciated."

### The one thing people want most

Remember, too, another axiom of this book: "Find out what people really want, and give it to them."

In telling me about the power of praise in business, Charles G. Nichols, told of a nation-wide poll conducted by the National Retail Dry Goods Association, of which he is a former president. Thousands of workers and bosses were asked to list, in order of their importance, the factors that they felt were of most importance to workers. "Credit for work" was the item that the workers themselves overwhelmingly rated number one. The bosses rated the same item seventh.

Evidently, few of us recognize just how very important it is to a worker to be given credit for the work he has done, to be accorded recognition and praised for a job well done.

People everywhere — in the home, school, office, plant, — are hungry for praise and appreciation. When we give them what they are hungry for, they are much more likely to be generous in giving us what we want from them, whether it is their skill, manual work, ideas, cooperation, or what not.

## How to perform a small miracle every day

Life itself is the real miracle. And every time you can give another person more life — or "put more life into him," as the common saying goes — you are performing a small miracle. Anytime you can give another person's spirits a lift, or imbue him with more life and energy, you are performing a small miracle. It's very simple. All you do is make it a practice to give genuine sincere praise to someone every day.

Try it on your wife, husband, child, boss, customer, or employee, and watch the other fellow immediately "perk up." Also notice how the other person automatically becomes more friendly and cooperative.

Also notice how your "small miracle" actually enables the other person to do better. Remember how psychologist Dr. Henry H. Goddard measured scientifically the increase in energy in school children when they were praised? It has also been proved that praise actually enables students to make better grades. When students were told just before an examination, "You will have little trouble with this test. It is well within your abilities and intelligence" they made better marks than when their intelligence and ability were run down just prior to the test. Praising their ability seemed to increase their ability.

American industry has also proved that honest praise, and giving credit where credit is due, not only makes workers *feel* better, but actually turn out more work. "Bonus systems" that just hand out money to employees, as a "gift" from the boss, invariably fail. But where bonuses and profit-sharing are based on merit, and as a means of recognizing a man's worth to the company, production always shoots up. Remember the story

about the workers at Lincoln Electric, in Cleveland, who produce up to 12 times as much as workers in comparable plants?
James F. Lincoln says that one big reason is that workers are
recognized and given credit for what they do.

### Be generous with kind statements

Don't wait until someone does something big or unusual to
praise him. Be generous with your praise. If your morning
cup of coffee is good, tell your wife about it. You'll not only
raise her spirits, but the chances are she'll try to brew the
coffee even better tomorrow morning.

If your stenographer gets out your letter faster than you had
expected, tell her so. She'll work even harder to please you.

If someone does you some small favor, show your appreciation
and give him credit for having done something by saying "Thank
you."

Look for things you can thank people for. Everytime you
say the words "Thank you," and mean it, you are giving the
other person credit — praising him for having done something
you appreciate.

Say those kind words. Let people know how you feel. Don't
take it for granted that they know you appreciate them: tell
them. When you let people know you appreciate what they
have done, it makes them want to do still more for you.

### Six rules for saying "thank you"

Those two little words, "Thank you," can be magic words in
human relations if they are used correctly. Memorize these six
rules. They have been tested and proved.

1. **Thanks should be sincere.**
   Say it as if you mean it. Put some feeling and life into
   it. Don't let it sound routine, but "special."
2. **Say it—don't mumble it.**
   Come right out with it. Don't act as if you were half-
   way ashamed for the other person to know you want to
   thank him.

3. **Thank people by name.**

> Personalize your thanks by naming the person thanked. If there are several people in a group to be thanked, don't just say "thanks everybody," but *name* them.

4. **Look at the person you are thanking.**

> If he is worth being thanked, he is worth being looked at and noticed.

5. ***Work* at thanking people.**

> Consciously and deliberately begin to look for things to thank other people for. Don't just wait until it occurs to you. Do it deliberately until it becomes a habit. Gratitude does not seem to be a natural trait of human nature. When Jesus healed ten lepers, only one thanked him. But are we very different?

6. **Thank people when they least expect it.**

> A "thank you" is even more powerful when the other person does not expect it, or necessarily feel that he deserves it. Think back to some time when you got a nice "thank you" from someone where it never occurred to you that any "thanks" were in order and you'll see what I mean.
>
> Not long ago a small boy came up to me on the street in Kansas City and asked me to buy a pencil. When I shook my head in the negative, he took me by surprise by saying (as if he really meant it) "Well, thank you very much, anyway, sir." Of course, I dug down in my pocket for a nickel. Watching him work his way up the street, I saw him sell half a dozen pencils before he got to the end of the block.

*A simple formula to boost your own happiness*

If you still have any lingering doubts that praise and gratitude have something akin to miraculous power in them, let me ask you this. If I told you about some man who possessed certain goods, and explained that the more he gave away the more he always had left . . . would you agree it was a miracle?

Well, that is what happens when you start giving away happiness and well-being to other people by praising them and thanking them. The more happiness you give away, the more you yourself have left.

Again, though science cannot explain it, psychologists and psychiatrists know it is true.

"The measure of mental health is the disposition to find good everywhere," said Ralph Waldo Emerson.

If you want to increase your own peace of mind and personal happiness there is no more certain formula than to start *looking for good* things in other people that you can praise. Start looking for good things in your life you can be truly thankful for.

Dr. George W. Crane, whose interesting syndicated column, "The Worry Clinic," appears in many newspapers, has shown thousands of people how to find happiness by joining what he calls "The Compliment Club."

The Club has no officers, club rooms, or formal meetings. Members merely agree to pay three sincere compliments to some person each day. They are not to wait until some person does something outstanding, or until they run up on some perfect person, but deliberately to go out and search for good things in other people that they can compliment.

This deliberate looking for the good things in others has a miraculous effect upon ourselves. It takes our minds off ourselves. Makes us less self-conscious. Less self-righteous. More tolerant and understanding. Dr. Crane says that this simple technique has literally worked miracles in curing his readers of all sorts of worry, fears, depression.

Several years ago, a number of psychologists got together to see whether they could come up with some one simple rule that would help people lead happier lives, with more peace of mind. They came up with a formula called SFF, which seemed to work miracles. The letters stand for "Stop Finding Fault."

One of the sure earmarks of virtually all neurotic, unhappy people, they found, was that they were overly critical. They deliberately looked for things to find fault with. Yet, when they changed their attitude, and began looking for *good* things in people around them and good things in their circumstances, their own happiness greatly increased.

No one is perfect. And it has been said that there is some good in everyone. Try an experiment. If there is some person who irritates you, or gets your goat, or keeps you upset, begin looking for something you can compliment him for. Even if he figuratively bites your head off — maybe he has nice teeth. If so, compliment him on his teeth. Keep on looking for things you can praise him about. Not only will he seem to change for the better; you'll find that your own opinion about him is changing.

## Two rules for administering praise

### 1. It must be sincere.

Mere flattery is easily seen through, and does nothing for either you or the other person. Remember there is always something *good* that *deserves* praise, if you'll look for it. It is much better to praise a person for some little something — and mean it, than to pick out something big, and be insincere.

It's much better, for example, to say to a woman, "You have the most beautiful hands I've ever seen," and mean every word of it, than to say, "You are the most beautiful woman in the world," if she isn't.

### 2. Praise the act or the attribute, rather than the person.

Praise a person for what he *does,* not for what he *is.* Compliment him on what he *has,* not on what he *is.*

RIGHT: Miss Smith, your typing lately has been truly excellent.
WRONG: Miss Smith, you are a good worker.
RIGHT: Jones, your sales led our entire district last week
WRONG: Jones, you're the best salesman we have.
RIGHT: You certainly have beautiful hair.
WRONG: You're a pretty person.
RIGHT: This is certainly a lovely house you have here.
WRONG: You must be a real big shot to live like this.

When you praise an *act* or *attribute,* your praise is specific and sounds more sincere. Also, best results are obtained if the other person knows *exactly* what he is being praised for. Praising the act rather than the person avoids charges of favoritism or prejudice. It also avoids embarrassment.

Most people feel ill at ease (or at least feel you are handing them a line) if you just walk up and say, "You're a great guy."

But if you pick out something specific he has done, he feels good about it.

Praising the act creates an incentive for the person being praised to do more of the same. Remember praise has a tendency to multiply and increase whatever it is aimed at. Praise a person for his work and he will do more work. Praise him for his behavior, and his behavior will improve. But praise him merely as a person and you only increase his egotism and conceit. Many a boy has been ruined for life by his mother constantly telling him, "You're the most wonderful person in the world." In fact, one reason most of us are so stingy with praise and compliments is the fear that we will give the other fellow a swelled head.

Praising a person's acts and attributes increases his feeling of self-esteem, which is a far cry from egotism and conceit.

Praising the other person, merely as a person, may very well make him conceited.

### CHAPTER 12 SUMMED UP

1. Sincere praise miraculuously releases energy in the other person, perks him up physically, as well as giving his spirits a lift.

2. The person who is discouraged, doing sloppy work, or just hard to get along with is probably suffering from low self-esteem. Praise can act as a wonder drug to give his self-esteem a healthy shot in the arm, change his behavior for the better.

3. Give others credit for what they do. Show your appreciation of what they have done by saying "thank you."

4. Be generous with kind statements. Gratitude is not a common thing. By being generous with gratitude, you make yourself a stand-out.

5. Increase your own happiness and peace of mind by paying three sincere compliments each day.

# Chapter 13

# HOW TO CRITICIZE OTHERS WITHOUT OFFENDING THEM

---

ABOUT 95 PER CENT OF THE TIME WHEN WE TELL another person, "I'm telling you this for your own good," we're not. We're telling him to bolster up our own ego by pointing out some fault in him.

One of the most common failings in human relations is the way that we (sometimes unconsciously) attempt to increase our own feeling of self-esteem by lowering the self-esteem of another person. Chronic fault-finding, belittling the other fellow, nagging, ripping the other fellow up the back, are all symptoms of low self-esteem.

As John D. Murphy expressed it in an article in *Your Life* magazine, "You have to be little, to belittle."

However, there are going to be times when the successful leader must point out errors and "correct" those working with him. This is truly an art, and one that most would-be leaders fall down on.

### Let's look at criticism in a new light

Because the art of criticism is so little known, and because 99 per cent of the people are so inept at it, the very word *criticism* leaves a bad taste in our mouths. When we think of the word, we think of those men and women who have criticized badly. We are apt to think of someone "jumping down our throat," "showing us up," humiliating us, beating us down.

137

However, the real purpose of criticism is not to beat the other fellow down, but to build him up. Not to hurt his feelings, but to help him do a job better.

Not long ago I was discussing the seven rules for successful criticism (which you will be given shortly) with Walter Johnson, vice-president of American Airlines. We were discussing the real need for criticism, and how it could be a real help.

"You know, Les," he said, "a pilot coming in for a landing is a good example of successful criticism. Frequently, his flying must be criticized or corrected by the tower. If he's off course, the tower doesn't hesitate to tell him so. If he's coming in too low, he's told about it. If he is going to overshoot the field, he is corrected. Yet I've never heard of one of our pilots getting offended by this criticism. I've never heard one say, 'Aw, he's always finding fault with my flying. Why can't he say something good for a change.'"

### How to keep the other fellow on the beam

The next time you must get someone back on the beam, remember how the airlines "correct" their pilots. Keep in mind that their criticism is not for the purpose of ego satisfaction, but to achieve a good end result for both the airline *and* the pilot. The man in the tower doesn't deal in personalities. He doesn't use recriminations. His criticism is not blared out over loud-speakers but in strict privacy to the pilot's earphones. He criticizes the act, not the person.

He doesn't say, "Well, if that isn't a dumb way to come in for a landing." He just says, "You're coming in too low."

The pilot isn't asked to do something merely to please the boss. He has a selfish incentive of his own to take the criticism and benefit by it. He is not offended; he actually appreciates it. He is more likely to buy the man in the tower a steak dinner than to cuss him.

And the really important thing is that both the pilot and his boss achieve some useful end result. The criticism accomplishes something.

All criticism could be given in the same spirit; if it were, equally good results would be achieved.

## The Seven Musts for Successful Criticism

### 1. Criticism must be made in absolute privacy.

If you want your criticism to take effect, you must not engage the other person's ego against you. Remember your goal — to achieve some good end result — or get him back on the beam. not to deflate his ego. Even if your motives are of the highest, and you have the right spirit about criticizing the other fellow, remember it's how *he* feels that counts. The mildest form of criticism made in the presence of others is very likely to be resented by the other person. Justified or not, he feels he has lost face before his co-workers or associates.

Whether you observe this rule or not is also a good indication of your real motives for criticizing. Do you criticize an employee only when you have an audience? Do you "correct" your husband's table manners in the presence of company? If so, the chances are very good that your real purpose in criticizing is not to help the other person, but to derive ego satisfaction out of humiliating him. Children are people, too. Insofar as it is possible, don't correct Junior in the presence of his playmates. Above all, don't preach him a sermon with others present.

### 2. Preface criticism with a kind word or compliment.

Kind words, compliments, praise, have the effect of setting the stage in a friendly atmosphere. It serves notice on the other fellow that you are not attacking his ego, and puts him more at his ease. The natural reaction of a person "called in on the carpet" is to get set to defend his ego. A person with this defensive frame of mind is not receptive to your ideas.

Clarence Francis, one of the founders of General Foods Corporation, said, "By praising a person you bring out the best in him, and he will understand you better when criticism is necessary."

Praise and compliments open the other person's mind:

> "Bill, that was a swell report you turned in. You certainly covered all the important factors. However, there was one thing. . . ."

> "Mary, you have done excellent work ever since you

joined our company. We appreciate your efforts along this line. There is one thought for improvement I know you would appreciate. . . ."

"Joe, you have always co-operated so well in the past. Is there any reason why. . . ."

"John, you certainly have been a good neighbor all these years. Do you know. . . ."

"I know from past experience that you are always looking for little ways to constantly improve your work. It occurred to me that. . . ."

**3. Make the criticism impersonal. Criticize the act, not the person.**

Here again, you can sidestep the other person's ego, by criticism of his actions or behavior, not his person. After all, it's his actions that you are interested in anyway. By pinpointing your criticism to his acts, you can actually pay him a compliment, and build up his ego at the same time:

"John, I know from past experience that this error is not typical of your usual performance."

"George, the only reason I mention this is that I know you can easily do better. It is not up to your usual high standard."

This way you actually build him up while pointing out his mistakes. Instead of telling him, "You're no good," you say in substance, "I think you're much better than this performance would indicate."

You let him know you think he is better than the error; that you expect him to do better. This in itself is a powerful incentive to "live up to" your expectation.

RIGHT:  "This word is misspelled."
WRONG: "Miss Jones, you are a terrible typist."
RIGHT:  "Better check your addition on these figures."
WRONG: "Of all the stupid mistakes."
RIGHT:  "Johnny, you must study harder and bring up this grade."
WRONG: "Why do you have to be so dumb?"

There may arise situations where it would be more diplomatic to point out the thing connected with a person, rather
than the act of the person himself. For example:

> "Fred, somehow or other the weekly report did not find
> its way up to the accounting office. (It is Fred's responsi-
> bility to send it up.) Do you know what happened to that
> report, Fred?" This rather than: "Fred, you didn't get the
> report up to the accounting office in time."

### 4. Supply the answer.

When you tell the other person what he did wrong — also tell
him how to do it right. The emphasis should not be on the
mistake, but the means and ways to correct the mistake and
avoid a repetition or recurrence.

*One of the biggest complaints of workers* is, "I don't know
what is expected of me. Nothing I do seems to please the boss,
but yet I am never sure what he wants."

Nothing can lower morale in an office, plant, or home, quite
so much as an atmosphere of general dissatisfaction without
there being any clear defining of just what is expected. Most
people are anxious to "do right" if you tell them what "right"
is.

As one worker expressed it to me, "My boss is always finding
fault, criticizing my work. All I know is my way of doing it is
'wrong.' Yet he never tells me what 'right' is. There is no
standard to aim at. It's like shooting at a target in the dark,
with no idea where the bull's-eye is. All I know is that regardless
of the direction I aim, I always seem to miss."

### 5. Ask for cooperation; don't demand it.

Asking always brings more cooperation than demanding.
"Will you make these corrections?" arouses much less resentment
than, "Do this over, and for Heaven's sake, this time see that you
get it right!"

When you demand, you place the other fellow in the role
of slave and yourself in the role of slave-driver. When you ask,
you place him in the role of a member of your team. Team feel-

ing, the feeling of participation, remember, gets much more cooperation than force.

It also makes a great deal of difference whether you put your criticism on the basis of "I'm the boss, and you'll do it this way because I say so," or whether you put it on the basis of, "Here's what we're shooting for, and here's how you can help achieve that goal."

You'll get much further if you give the other person a selfish incentive for *wanting* to change his actions, than if you merely issue an order that he do so.

It is generally conceded that National Cash Register Company, Dayton, Ohio, has one of the finest sales forces in the country. Ralph Negri, sales training director for National Cash Register, tells me that the secret of keeping salesmen on the beam is not to preach to them about what the company wants, but to give them an incentive to want to sell better.

Ralph never says, "You've got to do plenty of leg work if you want to work here." Instead, he is more likely to say something like, "If you force yourself to go out and make a few more calls, you can increase your income tremendously."

### 6.  One criticism to an offense.

To call attention to a given error one time is justified. Twice is unnecessary. And three times is nagging. Remember your goal in criticism: to get a job done, not to win an ego fight.

When you're tempted to drag up the past, or rehash a mistake that is over and done with, remember the illustration of how the man in the tower criticizes the pilot to bring him in safely. He tells him what he is doing wrong *now* and once that is corrected and settled, it is forgotten. Neither does the man in the tower "hold it against" the pilot because he once actually made a bad landing.

It is just as silly and ineffective for you to keep dragging up past mistakes and harping on them.

Employers are not the only ones who make this mistake. Husbands and wives drag up mistakes and errors from the past that should be dead and buried. Parents dig up dead issues in dealing with children. This never helps the other person to do better in the present; in fact, it is more likely to have just the opposite effect.

### 7. Finish in a friendly fashion.

Until an issue has been resolved on a friendly note, it really hasn't been finished. Don't leave things hanging in air, to be brought up later. Get it settled. Get it finished. Bury it.

Give the other fellow a pat on the back at the end of the interview. Let his last memory of the meeting be the pat on the back, instead of a kick in the pants.

RIGHT *(smiling)*: "I know I can count on you."
WRONG: "Now that you've been told, don't let it happen again."
RIGHT: "I know you'll get the knack of it—just keep trying."
WRONG· "You've either got to show improvement soon—or else!"

## *MEMORY JOGGERS FOR CHAPTER 13*

Remember that criticism, to be successful, must be for the purpose of accomplishing some worthwhile goal for both yourself and the person you're criticizing. Don't criticize just to bolster your own ego. And steer clear of the other fellow's ego when you must correct him.

Memorize these Seven Musts and begin to put them into practice:
1. Criticism must be made in absolute privacy.
2. Preface criticism with a kind word or compliment.
3. Make the criticism impersonal. Criticize the act, not the person.
4. Supply the answer.
5. Ask for cooperation—don't demand it.
6. One criticism to an offense.
7. Finish in a friendly fashion.

# Part Six

# YOUR HUMAN RELATIONS WORK BOOK

---

14. A Plan of Action That Will Bring Success and Happiness

# Chapter 14

# A SIMPLE, EFFECTIVE PLAN OF ACTION THAT WILL BRING YOU SUCCESS AND HAPPINESS

---

MOST SUCCESSFUL BUSINESSES TODAY HAVE ACTIVE human relations programs — not just libraries with books about human relations, but active, dynamic programs. They map definite plans to reach certain real-life goals. Then they start to work to reach those goals.

In this final chapter, let's get together and work out a personal "human relations program." Instead of just saying, "Well, I'll try to remember the advice in this book and see if I can get along better," let's set up some real goals to reach, and start off working toward them.

Whether you get anything out of this book, now, depends upon you. I have given you TESTED METHODS that have proved themselves in thousands of cases. I have given you knowledge about human nature that has proved itself time and time again. But knowledge *about* human relations is only one ingredient in the formula for your success and happiness. The formula goes like this:

**KNOWLEDGE + APPLICATION = SUCCESS**

You must supply the application.

## *The positive attitude will bring success*

First of all, a lot depends upon your reason for wanting to get along better with other people. If you try to apply the techniques in this book primarily as a means of *avoiding* trouble,

147

or *evading* friction, you are looking at human relations from a negative viewpoint. Not only are you keeping foremost in your mind the ideas of trouble and friction, and emphasizing to yourself how hard people are to get along with . . . just as important is the fact that such a negative attitude takes about all the zest and challenge out of improving your human relations.

You can't get very enthusiastic over such a negative program. you can't really put your heart into it if you feel that human relations is just a way of keeping your own desires and ego in check, so other people won't object, or if you think of "getting along with others" in terms of knuckling under to everyone, and letting everyone else have his way about everything.

Human relations can bring you both success and happiness. You should regard it as a skill that you are going to learn — a very rewarding skill. You should look forward to getting a real sense of satisfaction and a sense of accomplishment by improving your human relations. This positive outlook gives you an incentive to reach definite goals.

### Write down your objectives

One reason we don't secure any more improvement than we do from reading a book is that we never get right down to brass tacks and even consider how techniques and methods we read about can be applied to definite situations in our lives.

The knowledge contained in this book will do you little good unless you think of it in terms of your own experience, and your own problems. Writing down your objectives and goals has been found to be one of the very best methods ever discovered for impressing your goal on your mind, and helping yourself change your behavior.

So let's not let the knowledge you have learned from reading this book evaporate. Let's nail it down, by writing down your goals and objectives, and beginning to do something about them.

I have no way of knowing what your own problems or objectives might be. I do know, however, that most of us would like to improve our human relations in at least three areas of our lives: Our *work,* our *home life,* our *social life.*

So in keeping with the knowledge that a person becomes more enthusiastic and more willing to cooperate to achieve some goal if he is asked to participate, I am going to ask you to participate in the writing of this book. The goal I want to reach in writing this book is to help you improve your own human relations. But I need your help. I can't write in your objectives for you. If I could, I still couldn't tell *you* how to reach them as well as you can. So how about helping me out, and fill in the blank spaces on the pages to follow:

## MY HUMAN RELATIONS PROGRAM IN MY WORK

My Number One problem is................................................................

Page numbers in this book where information is given that will

throw some light on this problem are...............................................

Techniques and methods used by others in solving similar problems

are found on the following pages in this book..................................

Definite steps that I will put into practice immediately are:

1.  ..............................................................
    ..............................................................
    ..............................................................

2.  ..............................................................
    ..............................................................
    ..............................................................

3.  ..............................................................
    ..............................................................
    ..............................................................

4.  ..............................................................
    ..............................................................
    ..............................................................

5.  ..............................................................
    ..............................................................
    ..............................................................

Check-up date ....................[*one week later*]

Evaluation of          [   ] *Satisfactory, need more time.*

progress made:          [   ] *Unsatisfactory. need to change methods.*

In view of the results obtained during the past week, I now feel I should do the following: .................................................................

.........................................................................................

.........................................................................................

.........................................................................................

.........................................................................................

.........................................................................................

.........................................................................................

.........................................................................................

.........................................................................................

.........................................................................................

---

My Number Two problem is.................................................. ................

Page numbers in this book where information is given that will

throw some light on this problem are.................................................

Techniques and methods used by others in solving similar problems

are found on the following pages in this book...................................

Definite steps that I will put into practice immediately are:

1. ...............................................................

...............................................................

...............................................................

2. ...............................................................

...............................................................

...............................................................

3. ...............................................................

...............................................................

...............................................................

4. ...............................................................

...............................................................

...............................................................

5. ...............................................................

...............................................................

...............................................................

Check-up date ....................[*one week later*]

Evaluation of         [   ] *Satisfactory, need more time.*

progress made:        [   ] *Unsatisfactory, need to change methods.*

In view of the results obtained during the past week, I now feel
I should do the following: ........................................................

........................................................................................

........................................................................................

........................................................................................

........................................................................................

........................................................................................

........................................................................................

........................................................................................

........................................................................................

........................................................................................

––––––––––––––––––––

My Number Three Problem is........................................................

Page numbers in this book where information is given that will

throw some light on this problem are........................................

Techniques and methods used by others in solving similar problems

are found on the following pages in this book.................................

Definite steps that I will put into practice immediately are:

     1. ...............................................................

       ...............................................................

       ...............................................................

     2. ...............................................................

       ...............................................................

       ...............................................................

     3. ...............................................................

       ...............................................................

       ...............................................................

     4. ...............................................................

       ...............................................................

       ...............................................................

     5. ...............................................................

       ...............................................................

       ...............................................................

Check-up date ...................[*one week later*]

Evaluation of      [  ] *Satisfactory, need more time.*

progress made:      [  ] *Unsatisfactory, need to change methods.*

In view of the results obtained during the past week, I now feel I should do the following: .......................................................................

.......................................................................................

.......................................................................................

.......................................................................................

.......................................................................................

.......................................................................................

.......................................................................................

.......................................................................................

.......................................................................................

## MY HUMAN RELATIONS PROGRAM IN MY HOME

My Number One problem is...................................................................

Page numbers in this book where information is given that will throw some light on this problem are.....................................................

Techniques and methods used by others in solving similar problems are found on the following pages in this book...............................

Definite steps that I will put into practice immediately are:

1.  .......................................................

    .......................................................

    .......................................................

2.  .......................................................

    .......................................................

    .......................................................

3.  .......................................................

    .......................................................

    .......................................................

4.  .......................................................

    .......................................................

    .......................................................

5.  .......................................................

    .......................................................

    .......................................................

Check-up date ................[one week later]

Evaluation of          [  ] Satisfactory, need more time.

progress made:         [  ] Unsatisfactory, need to change methods.

In view of the results obtained during the past week, I now feel I should do the following: ................................................................

.............................................................................................

.............................................................................................

.............................................................................................

.............................................................................................

.............................................................................................

.............................................................................................

.............................................................................................

.............................................................................................

.............................................................................................

—————————————

My Number Two problem is................................................................

Page numbers in this book where information is given that will throw some light on this problem are................................................

Techniques and methods used by others in solving similar problems are found on the following pages in this book...................................

Definite steps that I will put into practice immediately are:

1.  ............................................................

    ............................................................

    ............................................................

2.  ............................................................

    ............................................................

    ............................................................

3.  ............................................................

    ............................................................

    ............................................................

4.  ............................................................

    ............................................................

    ............................................................

5.  ............................................................

    ............................................................

    ............................................................

Check-up date ....................*[one week later]*

Evaluation of          [  ] *Satisfactory, need more time*

progress made:        [  ] *Unsatisfactory, need to change methods.*

In view of the results obtained in the last week, I now feel I should do the following: ................................................................
........................................................................................
........................................................................................
........................................................................................
........................................................................................
........................................................................................
........................................................................................
........................................................................................
........................................................................................
........................................................................................
........................................................................................

---

My Number Three problem is................................................................

Page numbers in this book where information is given that will throw light on this problem are................................................................

Techniques and methods used by others in solving similar problems are found on the following pages in this book................................................................

Definite steps that I will put into practice immediately are:

1. ........................................................................
   ........................................................................
   ........................................................................

2. ........................................................................
   ........................................................................
   ........................................................................

3. ........................................................................
   ........................................................................
   ........................................................................

4. ........................................................................
   ........................................................................
   ........................................................................

5. ........................................................................
   ........................................................................
   ........................................................................

Check-up date ....................[*one week later*]

Evaluation of     [   ] *Satisfactory, need more time.*

progress made:     [   ] *Unsatisfactory, need to change methods.*

In view of the results obtained during the past week, I now feel I should do the following: ................................................................

........................................................................................

........................................................................................

........................................................................................

........................................................................................

........................................................................................

........................................................................................

........................................................................................

........................................................................................

........................................................................................

## MY HUMAN RELATIONS PROGRAM IN MY SOCIAL LIFE

My Number One problem is ...........................................................
Page numbers in this book where information is given that might throw some light on this problem are.............................................
Techniques and methods used by others in solving similar problems are found on the following pages in this book...................................
Definite steps that I will put into practice immediately are:

1. ..............................................................

........................................................

2. ..............................................................

........................................................

........................................................

3. ..............................................................

........................................................

........................................................

4. ..............................................................

........................................................

........................................................

5. ..............................................................

........................................................

........................................................

Check-up date ......................[one week later]

Evaluation of      [   ] *Satisfactory, need more time.*

progress made:     [   ] *Unsatisfactory, need to change methods.*

In view of the results obtained during the first week, I now feel
I should do the following: ................................................................

................................................................

................................................................

................................................................

................................................................

................................................................

................................................................

................................................................

................................................................

................................................................

---

My Number Two problem is ................................................

Page numbers in this book where information is given that might
throw some light on this problem are................................................

Techniques and methods used by others in solving similar problems
are found on the following pages in this book................................

Definite steps that I will put into practice immediately are:

1. ................................................................

................................................................

................................................................

2. ................................................................

................................................................

................................................................

3. ................................................................

................................................................

................................................................

4. ................................................................

................................................................

................................................................

5. ................................................................

................................................................

................................................................

Check-up date ......................[one week later]

Evaluation of          [  ] Satisfactory, need more time.

progress made:         [  ] Unsatisfactory, need to change methods.

In view of the results obtained during the first week, I now feel
I should do the following: ................................................................

................................................................................................

................................................................................................

................................................................................................

................................................................................................

................................................................................................

................................................................................................

................................................................................................

................................................................................................

................................................................................................

---

My Number Three problem is ..........................................................

Page numbers in this book where information is given that might
throw some light on this problem are.............................................

Techniques and methods used by others in solving similar problems
are found on the following pages in this book.................................

Definite steps that I will put into practice immediately are:

    1.  ........................................................

        ........................................................

        ........................................................

    2.  ........................................................

        ........................................................

        ........................................................

    3.  ........................................................

        ........................................................

        ........................................................

    4.  ........................................................

        ........................................................

        ........................................................

    5.  ........................................................

        ........................................................

        ........................................................

Check-up date ...................*[one week later]*

Evaluation of     [   ] *Satisfactory, need more time.*

progress made:     [   ] *Unsatisfactory, need to change methods*

In view of the results obtained during the first week, I now feel
I should do the following: ...........................................................................
......................................................................................................
......................................................................................................
......................................................................................................
......................................................................................................
......................................................................................................
......................................................................................................
......................................................................................................
......................................................................................................
......................................................................................................
......................................................................................................

## *Your Self-Improvement Program*

Benjamin Franklin tells in an autobiography how he tried
for years, with no success, to improve himself and rid himself
of certain habits. Then one day he sat down and wrote out a
list of what he considered to be his short-comings, such as bad
temper, impatience, lack of consideration for others, and the
like, and he picked out what he considered to be his number one
problem. Instead of just making a resolution to "improve himself," Franklin made an effort to work on his number one weak
spot. He took up his short-comings one at a time, and worked
on them *one at a time.* The end result was that within the
period of about a year he had overcome a great many bad habits
that had been holding him back.

Now I don't know what your faults are. And I wouldn't point
them out to you if I did. But, if you're reading this book that
means you're human. And if you're human, you have some
"bad" habits. When I use the words "bad habits," it's not in a
moral sense. It's not my job to try to make you "good." But I
speak of habits that are bad because they work against what you
really want. I am talking about habits that handicap you un-
necessarily in getting what you want from life.

I ask you to get rid of them, not from ethical or moral reasons,
but because they're like dead weights holding you back in the
game of life. Get rid of them, you'll find your progress towards
success and happiness much easier.

## A SELF-ANALYSIS CHECK LIST

|  | YES | NO |
|---|---|---|

1. Am I too critical of human nature? Do I expect other people to always be completely "selfless," yet expect them to give me what I want?  ☐ ☐

   ........................................................................
   ........................................................................
   ........................................................................

2. Do I expect everyone I deal with to be perfect, or do I make allowances and tend to give the other fellow the benefit of the doubt?  ☐ ☐

   ........................................................................
   ........................................................................
   ........................................................................

3. Am I willing to give the other fellow something he wants in return for something I want?  ☐ ☐

   ........................................................................
   ........................................................................
   ........................................................................

4. Everyone wants to increase his self-esteem. Do I satisfy my own self-esteem by legitimate accomplishment, or by trying to cut other people down to my size?  ☐ ☐

   ........................................................................
   ........................................................................
   ........................................................................

5. Am I genuinely interested in the other person and his problems?  ☐ ☐

   ........................................................................
   ........................................................................
   ........................................................................

6. Do I notice other people enough?  ☐ ☐

   ........................................................................
   ........................................................................
   ........................................................................

7. Do I accept other people as equals, or is there a slight ☐ ☐
   tendency towards self-righteousness or condescension?

   ........................................................................
   ........................................................................
   ........................................................................

8. Do I try to help the other fellow like himself better, ☐ ☐
   or do I try to deflate him?

   ........................................................................
   ........................................................................
   ........................................................................

9. Do I have respect for the other person's personality ☐ ☐
   and individuality?

   ........................................................................
   ........................................................................
   ........................................................................

10. Do I acknowledge respect for him and act in a way ☐ ☐
    that will make him feel important?

    ........................................................................
    ........................................................................
    ........................................................................

11. Do I assume that the other fellow will be friendly, ☐ ☐
    and take the initiative in meeting him more than
    half-way?

    ........................................................................
    ........................................................................
    ........................................................................

12. Am I careful enough in my appearance? Shoes ☐ ☐
    shined? Heels not run over? Hair cut? Clothes
    neatly pressed? Nails clean?

    ........................................................................
    ........................................................................
    ........................................................................

13. Do I myself show the attitude toward the other per- ☐ ☐
    son that I want him to show toward me?

    ........................................................................
    ........................................................................
    ........................................................................

14. Am I a good talker? An "easy-to-get-to-know" type □ □
of person?

...........................................................................

...........................................................................

...........................................................................

15. Do I listen attentively to other people? Do I listen □ □
enough?

...........................................................................

...........................................................................

...........................................................................

16. Am I skillful in getting my ideas across to others? □ □

...........................................................................

...........................................................................

...........................................................................

17. Am I successful in getting others to cooperate with □ □
me?

...........................................................................

...........................................................................

...........................................................................

18. When I ask others to help, do I allow them to par- □ □
ticipate? Do I give them a share in the profits if they
do participate?

...........................................................................

...........................................................................

...........................................................................

19. Do I make the most of the talents of those working □ □
with me by employing their brains as well as their
brawn?

...........................................................................

...........................................................................

...........................................................................

20. Do I know how to use the miracle power of praise? □ □
How long since I praised someone for something?

...........................................................................

...........................................................................

...........................................................................

21. Do I always give other people credit for what they do?   ☐  ☐
..................................................................................
..................................................................................
..................................................................................

22. How long has it been since I showed my apprecia-   ☐  ☐
tion by saying "thank you?"
..................................................................................
..................................................................................
..................................................................................

23. Can I criticize other people without making them   ☐  ☐
angry or hurting their feelings?
..................................................................................
..................................................................................
..................................................................................

24. Am I sincere in my dealings with others?   ☐  ☐
..................................................................................
..................................................................................
..................................................................................

25. Am I too impatient in dealing with people?   ☐  ☐
..................................................................................
..................................................................................
..................................................................................

26. Do I always give the other person some incentive —   ☐  ☐
some personal reason for doing what I want done,
or granting me a favor?
..................................................................................
..................................................................................
..................................................................................

27. Do I tend to hold grievances or grudges?   ☐  ☐
..................................................................................
..................................................................................
..................................................................................

28. Does my temper get me in trouble with others?   ☐  ☐
..................................................................................
..................................................................................
..................................................................................

29. Do I ever brag and bluster, or put on a big-shot act, ☐ ☐
    in order to hide my fears?

    ................................................................
    ................................................................
    ................................................................

30. Am I ever guilty of arrogance or snobbery?     ☐ ☐

    ................................................................
    ................................................................
    ................................................................

Items listed in the foregoing that I need to work on *now* are: Numbers ................................................................
    ................................................................
    ................................................................

Other items that need improvement are:

    1. ................................................................
    2. ................................................................
    3. ................................................................
    4. ................................................................
    5. ................................................................

References in this book that will help me improve on these points are found on pages number ................................................................
The first item I will work on will be
    No. 1 ................................................................
Definite steps I intend to take to improve this item are:

    ................................................................
    ................................................................
    ................................................................
    ................................................................
    ................................................................

### *YOU Must Write the End to This Book*

When I set out to write this book I had one purpose in mind. To help YOU, the individual reader, improve his own human relations and thereby get more happiness and success out of life. And as far as I am concerned the book won't be finished until that purpose is achieved.

So again, I need your help. For only *you* can finish this book.

When you have worked out your own human relations programs . . . when you have put them into practice, and proved them, and can write at the bottom of this page, "Mission accomplished," then this book will be ended.

I urge you, as a personal favor to me: don't leave my book unfinished. I don't like to be a failure, and I'll have failed in writing this book unless you step in and put these principles to work.

Resting on your library shelf they can accomplish nothing. Put into practice in your daily life, these principles can do for you what they have done for many thousands of others: bring success and happiness.